Classic

Football

Clangers

Classic Football Clangers

DAVID MORTIMER

ROBSON BOOKS

First published in Great Britain in 2004 by Robson Books,
The Chrysalis Building, Bramley Road, London W10 6SP

An imprint of Chrysalis Books Group plc

British Library Cataloguing in Publication Data
A catalogue record for this title is available from the British Library.

ISBN 1 86105 744 X

Typeset by SX Composing DTP, Rayleigh, Essex
Printed by Creative Print & Design (Wales), Ebbw Vale

Contents

This book is dedicated to the sizeable army of men and women who, weekly and (mostly) uncomplainingly, give up their time to help their offspring enjoy soccer. Running their own, and other people's, kids to and fro, training them, patching them up, washing their kit and helping the next generation in a hundred and one different ways.

The author has much for which to thank the British Newspaper Library for helping to flesh out detail or jog the memory. He has also had inspiration for one or two pieces from certain books that, if any football fan has not yet read, he thoroughly recommends: John Ludden's *Fields of Fire: The Greatest Football Matches Ever*, Nick Hazelwood's *In the Way! Goalkeepers: A Breed Apart?*, Colin Shindler's *Fathers, Sons and Football* and *Michael Parkinson on Football*. Last, but by no means least, he thanks his old friend John Clifton for searching his memory banks.

Foreword

Nobody old enough to remember the 1970s can forget the priceless moment when Gary Sprake, Leeds United's brilliant but eccentric goalkeeper, gathered the ball, made as if to throw it out and then, pirouetting like a discus thrower, hurled the ball with what seemed like a practised aim into his own net.

For months, and quite probably years, afterwards men were banging their pints down on the bar while they wiped away tears of laughter. Hilarious for us (provided we didn't follow Leeds United) and dreadful for Gary Sprake, who doubtless lost count of the number of total strangers he wished he could exterminate legally. Sprake was a good goalkeeper, good enough to play many times for Wales and make many brilliant saves, yet that one clanger is all too often the incident that is mentioned when his name comes up.

There's the rub. Which of us hasn't dropped the simplest catch at cricket, headed the ball into our own net, played an air shot on the tee or tripped over our own feet into the brambles to the unrestrained joy of the onlookers? We've all done it, and in all probability more than once or twice. Briefly, we feel a fool and then, if we're lucky and have a partner renowned for discretion, it's quietly forgotten.

But it's a different matter if you're a national player on a very public stage, playing in front of 10,000, 25,000 or 50,000 spectators, most of whom can feel the abnormal lightness in their wallets after forking out a second mortgage for the privilege of watching you. And, if you're one of the really big boys, those figures don't include half the nation's media and TV and radio commentators, all of whom will be only too pleased if you screw up à la Sprake so that they can practise their excruciating wit at your expense in sensational headlines. Which brings us neatly to the subject of this book.

To be more serious, one of the great attractions of sport is the interplay of human skill and emotion that it displays, and the way the participants rise or, sometimes, fall to the occasion; and the greater that occasion, the greater the pressure exerted on the players. Since soccer is a game concentrated into just ninety minutes, rapidity of thought and action is essential and, as fitness levels rise and technology improves equipment, the margins for error grow ever finer. Yet, as the media searchlight, television in particular, probes the game ever more insistently, the more a single failure of nerve, judgement, temperament or skill is exposed.

This little book celebrates some of soccer's red-faced moments drawn from 120 years or more of its history, and while it certainly puts names to most of the blushing faces, be they of individuals, teams or officials, it has absolutely no desire to shame them. Not only have most of them suffered enough already, but they were generally giving their all when the clanger was dropped, and in most cases those very same individuals or teams provided us with many more hours of pleasure than of cursing. Affection with, maybe, some occasional gentle humour is the order of the day!

It's Football, Des, But Not As We Know It

Getting the ball rolling, 1100 onwards

In one way, football is about the most ancient game we have. In another, it (or at least soccer) is the same age as rugby, and the laws of both games as we know them today evolved through a degree of trial and error towards the end of the nineteenth century. Way back in the twelfth century 'the famous game of ball' took place every Shrove Tuesday in London. Since several centuries were to pass before press and television arrived to persuade us that black is really white, we can only guess from second-hand accounts what mayhem this may have involved. Shrove Tuesday certainly seems to have been a day out for the lads, involving cock fighting, tavern brawls and a swaying mob of partially sober youths rushing around in pursuit of a round object. Come to think of it, only the cock fighting seems to have changed much.

Down the centuries, we keep stumbling across proclamations banning or otherwise lamenting this football thing. Edward II banned the 'sport' in London in 1314. Evidently he had as much impact as a modern politician, since Edward III tried again seventeen years later, tut-tutting about it as a public nuisance. Less than a century passed before Henry IV was imposing fines on this 'public misdemeanour'. So it went on but, little by little, those in authority evidently came to the conclusion that what can't be beaten must be joined.

In 1581, the headmaster of St Paul's School in London, while admitting football brought with it violence and abuse, reckoned that, since so many people enjoyed it, it must have some good qualities – if only he could find them. After much sucking of teeth, he decided it promoted health and strength, and suggested that a 'trayning master' at the school would be a smart idea. And so the very first ad for a games instructor was drafted and, in all probability, gave birth to the first referee.

Until the nineteenth century, the only constant in the game was that a round ball, whatever it might be made of, was at the centre of it. That round ball had to be got to some form of 'goal', which might be miles away or a matter of yards. How many people took part was a matter of local agreement, and just about anything – kicking, hacking, catching, throwing, manslaughter – was permissible. It was the Victorians, and in particular the great public schools that were becoming established, that began to impose order on the whole thing.

In 1841, Eton declared that football teams should consist of eleven a side. Other schools each introduced their own set of customs regulating the amount of kicking, catching and running that was allowed, but matters came to a head in the 1860s. The newly formed Football Association held a meeting to outlaw running, handling and mauling (as allowed at Rugby School) in favour of using the feet only (as insisted upon by Eton). The Blackheath Football Club was so outraged by this proposition and, in particular, its rider that banned hacking the shins of the player with the ball that it walked out in a huff. Thenceforth, Blackheath's version of the game was called Rugby, leaving behind the Eton version. 'Let's go down the park and play Eton' didn't have the right ring to it and so, mercifully, it came to be called soccer. Would you want to be glued to the World Eton Cup every four years, with the European Eton Cup cropping up betweentimes? Not forgetting our very own EA Cup every May?

Eton had said there must be eleven players a side, and so eleven there were. But what were they, and did they play 5–3–2, 4–4–2, 4–2–4, or whatever? No, they played 9–2. There were nine forwards and two behinds. Obviously. If you weren't forward, you must be behind, though to some clubs two behinds seemed a doubtful luxury. Since the object was to hoof the ball through the posts at t'other end, you naturally wanted as many strikers, or forwards, as you could muster.

Goalkeepers were an unwarranted luxury, and not until 1871 was such a position even recognised, never mind respected. There was, though, a rule in existence that allowed any player to catch the ball while simultaneously digging a mark in the turf with his boot, thus winning a free kick from the spot. This honourable tradition still exists in rugby, but, since soccer also had it in those days, what could be more natural than to transfer part of the concept, that of handling, to a single player?

This new-fangled goalie, a last-ditch defender, could handle the ball anywhere in his own half of the field – a luxury many of today's more adventurous custodians would clearly relish. (Not until 1912 were they imprisoned within the penalty area.) This in turn created the need for more precisely marked goals. A couple of posts weren't good enough, so a tape was strung across the top and then, in 1875, a proper bar. By 1891, the opportunities for endless argument were further diminished by hanging nets behind the posts but, almost simultaneously, the penalty kick was introduced, thus ensuring the pleasure of controversy for countless millions as yet unborn. (For passing interest, Mr McLuggage is credited with scoring the first official penalty goal.)

Which brings us neatly to the first soccer clanger, perpetrated by Lord Kinnaird in the FA Cup final of 1877 between Oxford University and Wanderers. Lord K, being a bit of an all-round sportsman, was very decently taking time away from his estates to turn out for Wanderers, as he liked to do when opportunity permitted. He didn't see himself as a behind, and certainly not as a goalkeeper, fancying himself as what would later be called a centre-forward – i.e. a striker. But, since no one else seemed prepared to do the job, he reluctantly agreed. Almost at once he wished he hadn't. Oxford had a shot from far out. Lord K gathered safely, and stepped back to survey the green acres ahead of him. Alas, he stepped back behind his line. There was an appeal, the umpires gathered in solemn conclave and pronounced it a goal.

Wanderers won, so the outcome was not affected, but Lord K felt the slight keenly. That he, whose role was to set an example to the less fortunate, should perpetrate an own goal was too much. He appealed to the FA, who, naturally, could feel nothing but sympathy for one of their own. A special meeting was called, and it was formally agreed that the umpires had been deficient in the matter of eyesight (not to mention judgement and respect for the nobility). Lord Kinnaird's bloomer was expunged from the official records – and, the world over, the less fortunate have ever since judged it acceptable to question the eyesight, legitimacy and allegiance of referees.

The Future King is Stunned

Preston North End v Wolverhampton Wanderers, FA Cup final, 1889

Once soccer began to get itself organised, Preston North End quickly established themselves as the team to beat and, in the season 1888–9, nobody could. The 'Proud Preston' tag was established and lasted for a good half-century and more. 'The Invincibles' was their alternative name, and, although Arsenal might lay claim to a similar title 115 years later, they merely went through the league programme (admittedly a much longer one) undefeated, their interest in the FA Cup being terminated in the semi-finals. Preston not only won the 1888–9 League Championship without losing, but also lifted the Cup without a single shot passing between the posts guarded by the splendid Dr R R Mills-Roberts. Had there been a European Champions Cup to win in those days they would probably have got their hands on that as well. Everybody knew, though – and if they didn't it was patiently explained to them – that any sport the British hadn't invented wasn't worth calling a sport. This made it obvious that if you were champions at home you were the best in the world and it was therefore pointless having other competitions.

Preston were hardly lacking in confidence in those days. They had reached the Cup final in the previous year, 1887–8, and were so certain of beating West Bromwich Albion that they arranged for a team photograph with the cup itself before actually bothering to go out and win it. They lost 2–1.

Their opponents, Wolves, in the 1889 Cup final at Kennington Oval therefore reckoned they had at least an even chance of engineering a similar surprise. Their tactics were straightforward. Rough 'em up a bit or, better still, a lot. They did their best, but the referee, Major Marindin of the Royal Engineers, was alert to this – admittedly according to the standards of the time, which were less squeamish than today's when it came to what constituted an acceptable challenge. In any case, the solid citizens from Preston were no shrinking violets themselves, and they carried the day 3–0.

Nineteenth-century equipment hardly encouraged the subtle flicks and gliding runs we routinely expect a century later. Boots were just that – boots. They were heavy and solid, as they needed to be to cope with a ball that could have done duty as a large-bore cannonball. Made of leather panels stitched together, the soccer ball of the nineteenth and early twentieth centuries became heavier and heavier as it absorbed moisture from the pitch. Kicking it, let alone unleashing a thunderbolt past the keeper, left no latitude for brittle bones or flabby muscles, and heading the thing was an act of courage that guaranteed a lasting headache.

The Prince of Wales, the future Edward VII, graced the final with his presence and was sitting alongside the Preston chairman, William Sudell. Even more than today, soccer was foreign territory for the future monarch, who was far happier on the grouse moors or playing cards with an attractive woman stationed somewhere en route to the bedroom. He gazed uncomprehendingly at the warfare going on before him, doubtless wincing from time to time as bone crunched on bone, or heavy leather thudded on flesh. Finally, as a player rose to head the ball, he could contain himself no longer. Turning to the Preston chairman he exclaimed in baffled astonishment: 'I say, Sudell, that man kicked the ball with his head!'

Thunderbolt Leaves Villa Thunderstruck

Aston Villa v West Bromwich Albion, FA Cup final, 1895

Timekeeping in the early days of organised soccer was pretty haphazard, so it's quite possible that some among the 42,000 crowd missed the business part of the 1895 Cup final. It was the first to be played at Crystal Palace, and it renewed an all-Birmingham Cup rivalry between Aston Villa and West Bromwich Albion that stretched back to 1887. In that year, Villa had beaten West Brom but, in 1892, the latter gained revenge in the last final to be staged at Kennington Oval.

Within thirty seconds of the kick-off, Villa had scored the only goal of the match – or, to be more exact, Villa had been credited with the goal, though nobody seemed to know quite what had happened or who should take the credit. The build-up to the goal was clear enough. Villa's centre-forward, Devey, played the ball to his inside-left; Hodgetts swung the ball across the field to outside-right Athersmith who floated over a pass that inside-right Chatt volleyed goalwards.

It went into the new-fangled net all right, but how it got there remained a puzzle. Something or somebody deflected it, but who or what? Had the West Brom keeper bungled his clearance? Had Devey got a touch on the ball? Or was it all an optical illusion, depriving Chatt of the honour? High-speed photography being as yet uninvented, an artist present tried to sort out the confusion for the help of next day's newspaper readers, but succeeded only in muddling the issue further. He portrayed what can only be described as a mess of West Brom and Villa players gazing skywards at a ball that appears to be six feet or more above the keeper's head and – unless spinning like a corkscrew – clearly going over the bar. Never mind. The goal stood, Villa fans immediately christened it the 'Crystal Palace Thunderbolt', despite its being quite obviously nothing of the sort, and Villa lifted the Cup.

So far, so good (or bad if you supported West Brom). It was what happened later in the year that hit Villa with the force of something much closer to a real thunderbolt. Proud of their achievement in winning the English Cup, as it was known for half a century until the Welsh unsportingly won it, Villa agreed to its being displayed in the window of a sports shop belonging to William Shilcock. 'Between the hours of 9.30 p.m. on Wednesday 11th September and 7.30 a.m. on Thursday, the 12th inst.' there was a gentle splintering of wood and there the Cup wasn't. Nor, as the report continued, was 'cash in drawer'.

The full majesty of Birmingham Police Force moved in with stately tread, and offered a reward of a tenner for information leading to its apprehension. Since the Cup itself was worth £25, without considering the amount of 'cash in drawer', there was a resounding silence. However far the long arm of the law groped, of the Cup there was no sign. Nor has there been from that day to this. For their slack security, naughty Aston Villa were required to fork out £25 to have a new Cup made. Five months after its delivery, the Crystal Palace Thunderbolt boomeranged pretty smartly to leave Villa thunderstruck.

'Allo, 'Allo, 'Allo! It's the Short Arm of the Law!

Blackburn Rovers v Liverpool, 1896

Now what was it we were talking about a bit earlier? Ah, yes, referees. Charlie Sutcliffe was just a little fellow in stature, but a tireless one by nature. He was a lawyer by profession, and a football lover for as many hours as he could contrive to rid himself of the law. He played for Burnley in its early years as a soccer club (as Burnley Rovers it was a rugby club until 1882), and became a referee by accident. He was in the stands to watch Burnley play Preston North End when he was invited to take the whistle, the official arbiter having failed to show. He presided over a defeat for his old club and, for the first of many times, left the ground with vociferous noises ringing in his ears indicating that his impartial judgements had not been fully appreciated. The powers-that-be thought he had the makings of a good ref, however, so he kept his whistle about his person.

In September 1896 he was in charge of Blackburn's home game against Liverpool. To say that Blackburn were on top for most of the game is something of an understatement but, as fast as the Liverpool goalkeeper fished the ball sorrowfully from the back of his net, Charlie awarded him a free kick. Fortunately for his chances of leaving Blackburn alive, the home team managed one goal that satisfied him, but the fact remained he disallowed six 'goals' in quick succession. As *Athletic News* commented, 'The fact that the ball was put into the net seven times for one goal is, I fancy, something like a record.'

Charlie's most celebrated feat was to escape the wrath of the Sunderland fans after their game with Small Heath. As soon as the game was over 'several hundred' Sunderland youths made for his dressing room with, recounted Charlie, 'no friendly intentions'. The road outside was in the process of being repaired, and several heaps of large stones were piled beside it. The police were pretty quick in those days. 'Allo, 'allo, 'allo, thought Inspector Watson, in charge of their presence at the ground, trouble's brewing. And so he thought up a cunning wheeze. Overlooking the fact that Charlie was a wee fellow, way below the required six feet for policemen, he draped him in an outsize police greatcoat, dropped a helmet over his ears and marched him out of the ground. Charlie, not surprisingly, presented a 'grotesque appearance', but he made it into a waiting horse-drawn cab before his pursuers cottoned on. He made his getaway – just – as the local youths pursued the cab down the road.

The only problem with this tale is that, each time Charlie told it in later life, the ground and the teams refused to stay in one place. He had a reputation as a great after-dinner storyteller. This was one of his favourites and, no doubt, he tailored it to his audience. So we cannot be sure that it really was the youth of Sunderland that wanted his blood. It may just as well have been Birmingham, Manchester or a number of other places.

The *Liverpool Echo* went so far as to print a cartoon of the great escape, but, as this was much later in his life, it cannot be claimed as contemporary evidence. Charlie survived, though, and it was as well he did. He was a tireless worker for the Football League and it was thanks to him, more than to any other individual, that – somehow – organised soccer kept going during the hard years of World War I.

Fatty Foulke Fingered in Fracas

Liverpool v Sheffield United, 1898

William Foulke, 'Fatty' to the world at large, was phenomenal by any standards – phenomenally good as a custodian of the sticks, quick, safe and agile – and phenomenally large. He was tall, he was bulky and he grew steadily bulkier. When Sheffield United pulled him out of the pits in 1894 at the age of twenty, he was merely well built, weighing in at 208 pounds or approximately 94 kilos. By the turn of the century he had passed the 20-stone (127-kilo) mark, but was still a growing lad. At the time he moved to Chelsea in 1905 he was 23 stone (150 kilos), and by the time of his death in 1916 he had topped 28 stone. What was remarkable was that despite this handicap, as most people would see it, he just got better and better as a goalkeeper.

The Arsenal (or more properly Woolwich Arsenal) goalkeeper of the day, James Ashcroft, wrote an improving tract in 1906 on the attributes needed by a goalie. 'He must not carry too much flesh,' he intoned portentously. OK, so flesh is out. Poor old 'Fatty'. But wait. Conscious that only just across the Thames at Chelsea a spectacular contradiction was performing weekly, Ashcroft hastily added, 'The old Sheffield United man is a law unto himself. Take a thousand men of Foulke's bulk and you would not find one to compare with him in the matter of rapid agility and action.'

Wrapped inside Fatty's ample frame was a genial character with a great sense of humour, perfectly capable of unexpected eccentricities. On one

11

occasion at Chelsea, the crowd was surprised, shall we say, to see him run onto the pitch wrapped in a large white towel because, he later explained, his jersey was the same colour as his opponents' shirts, and he couldn't find anything else to fit him. But since he was a large and successful man, there were, inevitably, those who saw it as their business to cut him down to size. It was a rough old game at the turn of the century, played by working-class folk, a good few of whom had come out of the mines, like Fatty himself. The laws gave little protection to keepers, who were at perennial risk of being bundled bodily into the back of the net, with or without the ball. While Fatty could more than look after himself, his temper could sometimes fray when he reckoned he was getting more than his fair share of the treatment.

Over at Liverpool, George Allan was a centre-forward of the robust kind, and when Sheffield United went to Anfield in October 1898 he and Fatty had one of their many memorable encounters. Fatty swore that off the field he and Allan were quite good friends. There may have been some who believed him, though they would probably have been outnumbered in a crowd at a nonleague match. Allan, it was said, had announced to his fans that he would 'knock Foulke into the back of the net' when they met.

At half-time, Sheffield United were 1–0 up but owed their clean sheet to the woodwork and Fatty's brilliant performance in goal. The second half saw frustration piled upon Liverpool frustration until, as Fatty cleared a shot, he was charged by Allan doing an impression of a bull in a Spanish ring. This was too much for Fatty. According to some, he picked Allan up and stood him on his head in the mud. Those with a poetic turn of phrase insisted he was bouncing him up and down like a rubber ball. Since the press always tells the truth, let us turn to the *Liverpool Football Echo*, which was, of course, utterly impartial. 'The big man, losing his temper, seized Allan illegitimately and turned him upside down,' it said.

The referee, mindful of the number of pitch invasions that occurred in those days – how times have changed – thought it prudent to award a penalty. That made it 1–1, and, after they had fought so valiantly, the wind went out of United's sails, and they lost.

Many years later Fatty, wearing a much-practised look of wide-eyed innocence, explained 'what actually happened'. It was like this, he said, daring anyone to clear his throat: 'Allan was a big strong chap and he bore down on me with all his weight. I bent forward to protect myself and Allan, striking my right shoulder, flew right over me and fell heavily. He had a shaking-up, I admit, but quite the worst thing was that the referee gave a penalty against us, and it cost Sheffield the match.'

So there you are. Another blind referee. And of course you believe every word of the explanation, don't you?

Frying Tonight – and Most Nights

Derby County fail to win the Cup, 1898–1903

Before we give goalkeepers a rest there is one more who deserves honourable mention in the catalogue of bloopers, and that's poor Jack Fryer of Derby County. Try as he might (and he had three attempts), he had the greatest difficulty getting his hands on the ball, let alone a cup winner's medal. Jack was a tall man, which made it inevitable that the correspondents of the day unfailingly referred to him as 'Derby's lengthy custodian' and, under normal circumstances – i.e. anything but Cup finals – he seems to have been a pretty good keeper. Derby certainly stuck with him over the years, though by the end of 1903 they must have been asking themselves if this had been the best of all possible decisions.

His first attempt at winning the Cup came against Notts Forest at Crystal Palace in 1898. Derby were overwhelming favourites, having disposed of Aston Villa, Wolves, Liverpool and Everton in the earlier rounds and, for good psychological measure, walloped Forest 5–0 in a league game a week before the final. On the big day, though, Forest sprang a surprise by playing half their team without moustaches, making them quicker and lighter than their opponents. They took the lead when 'Sailor' Capes drove the ball past the unsighted Jack Fryer. Derby equalised with a header by the 'legendary' Steve Bloomer (all references to Bloomer are at pains to make it clear that he was legendary, though they generally omit to say for what), and then Jack made his big mistake. Just before half-time,

14

Charlie Richards thumped the ball straight at the gallant custodian, who grasped it for a second, and then dropped it. Capes gratefully drilled it or, if you prefer, rifled it past him. Derby never recovered from the blow, and, although Forest were effectively reduced to ten men in the second half, they scored a third four minutes from the end.

Never mind. Derby were back at Crystal Palace the following year, 1899, and this time their opponents were Sheffield United with, joy of joys, Fatty Foulke in goal for them. The prospect of Fatty at one end and 'Derby's lengthy custodian' at the other was irresistible for 74,000 people, a record final crowd. At half-time Derby held a 1–0 lead and things were looking much more encouraging than in the previous year. But the legendary Steve Bloomer was missing golden opportunities to put them further ahead and, in the second half, United went on a scoring spree. The final score was 4–1, so Jack Fryer's record now read: Finals – 2; Goals conceded – 7; Medals won – 0.

Derby retired to the Midlands for the next four years to lick their wounds and then, in 1903, came bouncing back to Crystal Palace to meet the unfancied Bury, whose appearance in the final was as unexpected as, say, Milwall's in 2004. The legendary Steve Bloomer was injured, but on paper Derby had a strong side nevertheless. On the day 'shambles' would be a polite description of their performance. They were thoroughly inept and thoroughly outplayed, so much so that the most energetic moment enjoyed by 'lengthy Jack's' opposite number, Monteith, in the Bury goal, was when he collected his winner's medal. Poor old Jack Fryer's third and last attempt at glory was terminated after a collision with Sagar as Bury launched a four-goal blitz in a twenty-minute assault. 'He stuck gallantly to his post' for a while before retiring, both bloodied and bowed. Bury's 6–0 win still stands as a record. Jack's Final record thus stood at: Finals – 3; Goals conceded – 13; Medals – 0. Derby did manage to lift the Cup in the end, but not until 1946, by which time Jack had lost all interest in proceedings.

Mr Kingscott Tries to Rewrite Twentieth-Century History

Sheffield United v Tottenham Hotspur, FA Cup final, 1901

It's a well-known fact – at least in North London – that throughout the twentieth century God so arranged things that Spurs would win the Cup at twenty-year intervals in years ending with the figure 1, provided the sum total of the figures in the year added up to an odd number.

If that sounds a bit complicated, it's simple for Spurs fans, who are brought up to understand the formula even as they imbibe their mother's milk. Thus, Spurs won the Cup in 1901, 1921, 1961 and 1981 and would, obviously, have won it in 1941 but for Hitler's underhand attempt to seize it for himself. The pattern was established when, as a Southern League side, they lifted the trophy for the first time in 1901, but it so nearly came to nothing because of Mr A G Kingscott, a referee who clearly had no understanding of preordained destiny, and no feeling for the symmetry of history.

The 1901 final attracted 110,000 to Crystal Palace, and they packed into every available square inch of standing space or, in many cases, dangled hopefully from the branches of trees with a view. Their opponents, Sheffield United, with the fabled Fatty Foulke, now up to 22 stone (140 kilos), in goal (see page 11), were the favourites. They had disposed of the mighty Aston Villa in the semi-final, and they showed their class as they swept into the lead with a goal from inside-left Priest in the eleventh minute. Midway through the first half, Spurs' centre-forward, Brown, gave Foulke no chance with a header, and from then on the London side began to play with a speed and intelligence that United struggled to contain.

Five minutes into the second half, Brown unleashed a magnificent shot that was still rising as it hit the back of the net, and it began to look as though the Cup was heading for Spurs' trophy cabinet. Mr Kingscott, though, was merely biding his time, and within sixty seconds he struck. United's left-winger, Lipsham, attempted either a cross or a shot. Whatever it was, Bennett charged goalkeeper Clawley, who managed to scramble the ball behind for a corner, duly signalled by the linesman. Mr Kingscott, gasping for air as he hurried goalwards from the distant upfield spaces, wasn't having that. To him, it was as clear as daylight. The ball must have crossed the line before Clawley palmed it past the post and it was therefore a goal – 2–2. History does not record how many spectators fell out of the trees in their indignation, but Mr Kingscott's decision stood, and the final finished as a draw.

The replay took place at Burnden Park, Bolton, on a wet and windswept day that discouraged all but a handful more than 20,000 from paying at the turnstiles. Luckily for predestination, Spurs won decisively, 3–1, and there was therefore no need for their supporters to indulge in a ritual burning of Mr Kingscott's effigy every twenty years, provided the year ended in a 1 and the sum total . . . Well, you've got the idea by now, I'm sure. It would only be a few more years before the Football League was expressing its grave concern about the physical fitness of its match officials, and sending out warning directives to anyone with a penchant for dressing in black on a Saturday afternoon.

The Most Outrageous Enterprise Ever to Be Conceived in English Football

Arsenal 'elected' to the First Division, 1919

Once upon a time, before even Granddad can remember, there was the Southern League (mere upstarts) and the Northern League (who called themselves the Football League, because it was well known – in the North – that soft Southerners were big girls' blouses and couldn't play a man's game like soccer). Woolwich Arsenal, though, joined the Football League early on, whereas Tottenham didn't get round to it until 1908. Whereupon Woolwich Arsenal promptly announced that the crowds weren't good enough south of the river, moved lock, stock and barrel to north London and put it about that under the skin they had always been just plain Arsenal. Surely, they probably said, everybody knew the good old North London chant 'One–nil to the Arsenal'.

Well, there you are, then. But Spurs and Clapton Orient reckoned nobody else should tap into support north of the Thames and immediately threw their toys out of the pram in all directions, complaining it wasn't fair and there weren't enough weekly sixpences to go round three teams in north London. The Football League said there were, and that, from 1909 on, was that. So, when the next row flared up ten years later, there was what you might call a bit of previous between Spurs and Arsenal.

The Arsenal chairman was Henry Norris, who was knighted in 1916, a fact of which the Football League was immensely proud. Just fancy, soccer was now such a respectable game that it had a Sir on its committee – and, what's more, a Sir who was also an MP and mixed with jolly useful people at Westminster. But come the end of World War I Sir Henry was in a bit of a fix. He'd ploughed an awful lot of money into building Arsenal's new stadium at Highbury and, what with the interruption of the war and everything, he hadn't had a penny back on all that money. He needed Arsenal to be successful, and as quickly as possible.

There was a slight problem. In the last season before the war, Arsenal had been only fifth in the Second Division, and you didn't get the big crowds to watch Second Division then, any more than you do today. Spurs, on the other hand, had been in the First Division, though admittedly bottom of it, immediately behind Chelsea. If the normal rules of two down, two up were applied, both Chelsea and Spurs would join Arsenal in the Second Division with every danger that *all* the London clubs would be disaffected and form a breakaway London League, financed by Sir Henry Norris. As the Southern League was withering away, anything that provided an alternative to the authority of the Football League would be a disaster. Right, lads – or, rather, right, Sir Henry – how shall we get out of this one?

Simple, really. Square Chelsea first of all, by finding a reason for them to stay up. This was fairly easy, since Manchester United had only just edged ahead of them in the 1914–15 season as a result of a rigged game with Liverpool. It hadn't been the club who fixed the match, but 'outside influences' who, in the fog of war, had never been fully identified. To send Chelsea down when everyone knew they were innocent victims would have been an outrage. So the 'two down' rule was suspended, and Chelsea were clear to declare their undying loyalty to the Football League.

That left the problem of the bottom place, and this was to be decided by the voting members of the Football League at their meeting in March 1919. Sir Henry was in his element. First, he was a good pal of the president of the League, 'Honest John' (really?) McKenna. Secondly, he had given great help to the League during the war and, to some extent, ensured its continuing existence. Finally, he was an adept fixer and lobbyist. So, when the crucial ballot came, the two top teams were Arsenal and Spurs, requiring a second ballot after the other teams, with fewer first-time votes, had been eliminated. The president, Honest John, stood up and made it clear that, in his view, there should be only one winner of the second ballot – Arsenal. Guess who won, by eighteen votes to eight. 'Everyone was afraid of Sir Henry,' wrote Leslie Knighton, one of Arsenal's later historians, 'and no wonder. I have never met his equal for logic, invective and ruthlessness.'

Spurs' riposte was immediate. They won the Second Division championship in 1919–20 and the FA Cup (for the second time) in 1921. They also finished above Arsenal in both 1921 and 1922. Arsenal are the only club ever to be promoted to the First Division without playing their way there – and, however they got into it, they are the only club never to have been relegated from it. The real loser was the Football League itself, having shown itself to be at the mercy of a powerful financier and politician. Sir Henry, mind you, got a kind of comeuppance. Although nothing at the time, or subsequently, has ever come to light suggesting money passed hands in 1919, he was banned from football eight years later for 'financial irregularities' and was refused admission to boardrooms around the country.

Preston Wait Mutch Too Long to Get Even

Huddersfield v Preston North End, FA Cup finals, 1922 and 1938

Proud Preston they were always called, and in football's early years they had plenty to be proud about. And in their middle years as well, come to that, for in the 1940s and 1950s they had Tom Finney, one of the greatest footballers of any time or place. In the 1922 Cup final played, for the last time before Wembley opened its gates, at Stamford Bridge, they were up against Huddersfield Town. Huddersfield were managed by Herbert Chapman, and it was on the strength of his achievements there that he was lured to Arsenal, whom he transformed into the leading team of the early 1930s.

It was a poor final. Each side seemed willing to go to almost any length to snuff out a hint of creativity by the other. The referee pranced around wagging the occasional finger but otherwise failing to exert his authority and, inevitably, the more he let go, the rougher the game became. In the end, his patience snapped and he awarded Huddersfield a penalty, but a highly controversial one. Billy Smith, Town's outside-left, was brought down from behind on the edge of the penalty area, and the referee pointed to the spot. Smith himself took the kick. Preston's goalkeeper, J F Mitchell, wiped his spectacles nervously, put them back on and bounced up and down on his line like a yo-yo, yelling and waving his arms, in an effort to distract Smith, but to no avail.

It was the first Cup final to be decided from the penalty spot. Unfortunately, the offence had almost certainly taken place outside the area. The skid marks left in the turf made it pretty clear Smith had been felled *outside* the area before tumbling gracefully *into* it. Preston retired to Lancashire and brooded darkly for the next sixteen years.

In 1938 their chance for revenge came as they returned to Wembley to face Huddersfield again. The players, of course, were completely different, but the sense of injustice lingered all the same. Just as in 1922, it was a dull, colourless match, made worse for the spectators by the fact that at the end of ninety minutes there was no score and another thirty minutes of additional tedium beckoned. Extra time was, indeed, no better, and many in the 93,000 crowd thought longingly of tea and toast at home and made for the exits.

There were only ninety seconds left when George Mutch, Preston's inside-right, set off, ball at feet, in the direction of Huddersfield's goal. Like a Red Sea confronting a latter-day Moses, the defence seemed to open before him. Until the science of sports nutrition and training began to be better understood and applied in the 1970s, it was received wisdom that the Wembley turf sapped your stamina. Nobody had the energy left to challenge Mutch until he was inside the penalty area. Then, a despairing tackle came in from centre-half Young, and Mutch crumpled like discarded paper. He may even have been grateful to be felled. It gave him time to summon up the strength to hit a shot. He took the penalty himself. It was straight, hard and high. Hitting the underside of the bar it flashed downwards into the net, and Preston felt themselves avenged.

Ernie Barlow Pockets the Evidence

Stockport County v Stoke City, Division 3 (North), 1927

Ernest Barlow was a devoted chairman of Stockport County, if a little unpredictable and autocratic, and he was keen for his lads to scale the ladder of Division 3 (North) and leap onto the dizzy peaks of Division 2. There was a crucial game in prospect against Stoke City, their great rivals for the spot, top, promotion, for the winning of. Ernie formed a very cunning plan. Down the road at Bolton Wanderers, the teeth of the colourful Joe Smith were getting a bit long, suggesting that his owners – i.e. Bolton – might be open to negotiations for his transfer. Joe had been capped five times by England, was famed for his weight of shot and had been an FA Cup winner, twice, in 1923 and 1926. Not only might he add to Stockport's attacking strengths, but he'd attract higher takings at the gate. So Ernie sidled along to Bolton.

It all went like clockwork and, sure enough, Stockport recorded their highest-ever takings for the home game against Stoke in March 1927. The result was a 2–2 draw and satisfaction all round – until the truth came out. Joe Smith could play only once he had been properly registered with the Football League, and before the game started our Ernie had received a telegram informing him that Smith's registration had not yet gone through. Deciding that what he couldn't see he didn't have to think about, he stuffed the telegram in his pocket and forgot about it.

It wasn't long before the news of Smith's contribution to the fighting draw with Stoke came to the attention of the League, and there is nothing like an official body's umbrage when its words have been ignored. Stockport had two points deducted, which torpedoed their hopes for the bright lights of Division 2 *and* they were fined the then considerable sum of £100. Stoke were promoted at the end of the season and Stockport didn't escape from Division 3 (North) until World War II was looming on the horizon.

There'll Be Bluebirds Over the Twin Towers of Wembley

Arsenal v Cardiff City, Cup final, 1927

Ninety-one thousand poured into Wembley Stadium, a state-of-the-art arena hosting its fifth final, to see norf London side Arsenal, the Gunners, take on Cardiff City, the Bluebirds, from Wales. Wales? That couldn't be right. This was the *English* Cup, dammit. How could a Welsh team have got in on the act? But they had, by beating Reading in the semi-finals, and partly as a result of the outcome of the Wembley encounter, the English Cup became, and remains, the FA Cup.

As the City players made their way to the stadium they passed thousands of their supporters happily singing 'I'm Forever Blowing Bubbles', not yet a tune appropriated for the sole use of West Ham. So great were the crowds that the Gunners made it to their dressing room with only thirty minutes to spare. They were skippered by the England international and World War I hero Charlie Buchan, 'the greatest player I ever saw', according to Bill Ditchburn, the former chairman of Sunderland. Before kick-off, the teams lined up to be inspected by King George V. Cardiff's Ernie Curtis said afterwards that the king mumbled something indecipherable to him, but over the years he developed the tale until George V had said to him, 'Hello, Ernie, how are you?', to which Ernie had replied, 'Fine, George. See you after the game.'

All nice and relaxed in retrospect but, reflecting the fact that neither team had reached the Cup final before, the match itself was tense and nervy. Arsenal did most of the attacking, but Cardiff's strength lay in the rocklike defence of Hardy, Sloan, Nelson and Watson, marshalled by their captain Fred Keenor. Seventy-three minutes had gone and both goals remained virgin when, on one of Cardiff's occasional forays into the heart of the Arsenal defence, Hughie Ferguson shot from twenty yards. In later retellings, the shot was described as a weak, speculative effort that bobbled towards Dan Lewis, Arsenal's Welsh goalkeeper, who allowed it to slide under his body on the greasy surface as he went down to save it. It was the only goal of the match and, for the one and only time in the Cup's history, the trophy vanished over the borders for twelve months.

That was not how it really happened but, as we see daily in the modern tabloids, people love to make a tragedy out of a misfortune. Ferguson's shot was a good one and, as Keenor said later, 'The quality of Lewis was shown by the fact that he stopped the shot in the first place. A second-rater would not have seen it, but Lewis made a mighty effort.' Lewis gathered the ball, but as he got up his knee hit it and pushed it behind him. He turned to fall on it before it spun over the line, but succeeded only in nudging it backwards and, with agonising slowness, it trickled into the net. It was still an impressively deafening clanger, but another equally sonorous one had yet to happen.

Arsenal had a great chance to equalise when Sid Hoar crossed from the left and cleared the head of the Cardiff goalie. The ball bounced between Buchan and Jimmy Brain in front of an empty net, but in a show of excessive politeness each left the glory of a Wembley goal to the other and let it bounce its way across the penalty area, probably chuckling to itself as it did so. 'I did not have a good game,' said Buchan with unnecessary candour afterwards. However disappointed he and his team were, it didn't stop him and Billy Blyth joining the Bluebirds in their dressing-room celebrations once George V had handed over the Cup from the royal box.

These celebrations were as nothing to what went on back in Cardiff. The final was the first to be broadcast on radio, and thousands turned out to listen to it live in Cathays Park. Hundreds of thousands turned out to welcome the team back as they paraded the Cup through the streets aboard a double-decker bus, and it wasn't 'Bubbles' they were singing this time but 'Land of my Fathers'. 'Such a welcome as this is an even greater triumph than our victory at Wembley,' said Len Davies. Billy Hardy, the hero of the game who had needed a police escort to save him from the invading fans as he struggled towards the royal box for his medal, said simply, 'I am quite content.'

Back at Wembley, poor old Arsenal had had six bottles of champagne on ice. Eventually they recovered enough to contemplate drowning their sorrows, but the more they looked for the champagne the more they couldn't find it. The dressing-room attendant had nicked the lot. Clanger number three!

Time to Draw a Line Under the Matter

Arsenal v Newcastle United, FA Cup final, 1932

There was only ever one winner of the 1932 final – until it was played. Arsenal, cup-holders in 1930 and now well and truly embarked on their glory years under their first great manager, Herbert Chapman, had finished second in the League. Newcastle, for all the passionate support of the faithful Tynesiders, had looked a pretty average team for most of the season. To be sure, Arsenal were without their injured playmaker Alex James, he of the diminutive stature and famously baggy shorts, but this was, surely, a minor disadvantage. With their impregnable defence and famous front five of Hulme, Jack, Lambert, Bastin and John, one would hardly notice he was missing – or so the fans consoled themselves.

Sure enough, after fifteen minutes Arsenal were ahead. Centre-half Roberts, known as the 'Police Constable' for the way he shackled the opponents' attack, sent a long pass out to Joe Hulme on the left wing, whose perfectly weighted cross eluded McInroy in the Newcastle goal, to leave Jack with an open goal. In the previous nine years of Wembley finals, the team scoring first had gone on to win, so the crowd settled back to wait for the next goal. When it came, after 38 minutes, it wasn't at the expected end. It was to become one of the most celebrated and most disputed goals in Wembley history. United's inside-right, Richardson, took the ball outside his marker to the dead-ball line – and over it – before hooking it back into the penalty area. The Arsenal players, seeing the ball cross the line, checked and began to turn upfield, expecting a goal kick to be given. It was enough for centre-forward Allen to outjump Roberts and score with his head. In an atmosphere of increasing tension the second-half swayed back and forth, but the destiny of the Cup was settled thirteen minutes from time, when Allen scored again.

There are at least two photographs of Richardson's notorious cross, taken parallel with the goal line at the moment of impact, and showing the ball clearly over the line. All three match officials appear in one of the photos. The referee, one Percival Harper (Percy to his friends, of whom he was about to shed a large number), is three or four yards outside the penalty area, directly facing the goal. 'I was eight yards away,' he later claimed, revealing a deficiency in the memory department as well as the eyesight. The linesman on Richardson's side of the field is nearer the halfway line than the penalty area, at far too great a distance to see the incident. His opposite number is better positioned, two or three yards inside the edge of the penalty area but, of course, on the far side of the field.

Given their positions at the time of the cross, it's clear none of the officials could have been aware that the ball had gone dead by an inch or two. Whether they were in the ideal positions, given where the play was taking place, is another matter, especially in the case of the linesman on Richardson's side. 'As God is my judge, the man was in play,' referee Harper continued stoutly to insist, and, when the photos were printed displaying the evidence of his own absence from the scene of the crime, he was not to be budged an inch. 'I do not mind what other people say,' he growled.

Today, of course, the 'we wuz robbed' laments would be the stuff of nightly replays on TV, the tabloids would have rummaged through the dustbins of the linesman to see what light they could shed on the poor fellow's morals and eating habits and Richardson would have bought a house in Spain after doing a shoot for *Hello!* magazine. In 1932 there was little option but to get on with life, though a sense of injustice pervaded north London – or at least the Arsenal half of it – until well after World War II was done and dusted.

Chapman is Made to Look a Bit of a Herbert

Walsall v Arsenal, FA Cup, 3rd round, 1933

Some Cup shocks are more shocking than others. We never tire of reminding ourselves that it's the unexpected that makes the FA Cup so compelling. When Yeovil Town beat the (then) mighty Sunderland on their infamously sloping ground in 1948 it rocked sports fans everywhere. Hereford, York City, Sutton, Tranmere and Dag & Reds all have honoured places among those who have cocked a few warmly applauded snooks in the faces of the high and mighty.

But probably no Cup upset ever produced the impact achieved by Walsall in their third-round tie in 1933. They were drawn against the very mighty Arsenal, fresh from the imposing marble halls of Highbury. Herbert Chapman was the first of the super-managers, a mastermind who, like Clive Woodward with the England rugby team seventy years later, thought of every little detail, from playing skills and tactics to what the players ate. The results were sensational. Throughout the 1930s Arsenal were *the* team to beat. They won the Cup in 1930, were runners-up in highly controversial circumstances in 1932 (see page 28) and if a year passed in which they were not champions it aroused the suspicion that God's attention had momentarily wandered.

Chapman chose the tie with lowly Walsall to try out two new forwards then learning their trade – though not very well, it has to be said – in the reserves. One was right-winger Billy Warnes; the other a centre-forward, Charlie Walsh, who tended to get a bit tense when asked to perform at the highest level. Or, indeed, at quite a low level, as the Walsall tie was to demonstrate.

Everything that *could* go wrong for Arsenal *did* go wrong, and quite a lot of it went wrong for poor old Walsh in particular. He missed four chances, including a sitter in front of an open goal from a cross by Cliff Bastin. Rather than put his head in the way of a leather ball that tended, in those days, to be big and heavy, he let it hit him on the shoulder. He then compounded his error by obstructing his own teammate, the famous David Jack, just as he was about to pop the ball in the net. Result: 2–0 to Walsall. Over two generations later, it's almost impossible to understand the cataclysmic effect this result had on people who, in those pre-TV days, relied on the Saturday night sports paper, the *Green 'Un*, to bring them the soccer scores. Today it would be a little like, say, Cowdenbeath beating Real Madrid, or a worm giving a blackbird a pair of black eyes.

Writing in *The Times*, Brian Glanville was reminded of Chapman's clanger by a couple of equally dire decisions towards the end of the 2003–4 season by another famous Arsenal manager, Arsène Wenger. Ten minutes from the end of their home league game with Manchester United at the beginning of April, Wenger brought on Patrick Cygan to bolster the defence and protect a 1–0 lead. No doubt he was mindful of the Cup semi-final with United at Villa Park a few days later but unfortunately, as Glanville said, Cygan was 'an accident waiting to happen', and he was also being played out of position. From being wholly in control, Arsenal surrendered the initiative, United equalised and, perhaps for the first time that season, saw that Arsenal were fallible. It made little difference to their league positions, but psychologically, with the Cup semi-final ahead, it was foolish. Yet Wenger compounded the mistake by keeping his two outstanding strikers, Thierry Henry and Antonio Reyes, on the bench for the opening of the tie. Manchester United's somewhat unpredictable defence was given time to settle down, and they won the semi-final 1–0 to leave Arsenal fans feeling even less well than a flock of birds with colourful feathers.

Oh, Oh, Oh, Oh, Oh What a Lovely Pools War!

Moral rectitude and the Football League, 1936

To gamble or not to gamble, that is the question. Whether 'tis nobler to suffer Pools in silence or take arms against a sea of coupons and by opposing end them. Roughly speaking, that was the dilemma facing the worthies of the Football League in 1936. Three years earlier, there had been a Royal Commission on Lotteries and Betting that had managed to leave soccer out of the equation, and by 1936 the revenue from the relatively new pools companies had become significant. Whereas gate receipts from football matches were about £48,000 a week, the money spent on pools was reckoned to be £800,000, nearly seventeen times as much.

The pools companies made tentative approaches to the Football League to pass on a percentage of the loot but, strapped for cash as they were, the moral majority on the committee, headed by none other than Charlie Sutcliffe (see page 9), was quite clear where its duty lay. 'There can be no connection, however vague, between the League and betting,' it intoned.

Despite the elevation of the League's nose, and the arctic temperature of its icy stare, the issue refused to go away, so the League devised a plan of such cunning that Blackadder himself would have been rendered speechless. The pools companies depended on printing and mailing the list of fixtures a week or so ahead of the time the games were to be played. Was it not so? It was indeed. Very well, the League would scrap the existing fixture list and simply announce who was playing whom the day before it was due to happen. The pools companies would then be unable to print and dispatch their coupons in time, and would go bankrupt. The nation's soul would be saved and the problem solved. Brilliant!

Admittedly there were one or two minor flaws. Who, for example, owned the copyright in the table of Football League fixtures? Did the League have the legal right to play fast and loose with it in this way? And what about the fans? Surely they would rather like to know if they were going to watch a local derby or that well-known bunch of cloggers from, well, from wherever. And if they followed their team to its away games it would help to know if they had to look up train times to Darlington or Plymouth, say.

Details, my dear fellow, don't bother me with mere details. Look at the bigger picture.

So, it was duly announced that the Pools War would start on Saturday, 29 February. In strict secrecy, the Football League would tell the chairmen of the clubs in advance whom they were to play come Saturday, but there would be no public announcement until 24 hours before.

It was, of course, a disaster. Details were leaked to the press by many of the clubs; the pools companies issued blank coupons with instructions to look for later announcements in the press about how to fill them in; and the fans voted with their feet. Attendances were down almost everywhere: Newcastle United's average gate fell from 22,000 to 8,000; Leeds United and Liverpool suffered drastically reduced gates; Sheffield Wednesday had their smallest crowd of the season.

Of the 44 First and Second Division clubs, 36 met in Leeds to demand a restoration of the status quo. Politicians joined the fray, dividing across party lines. 'The football pool is the poor man's little flutter,' said the sympathetic ones. Others saw it 'not as a little matter, but as a gambling craze'. Just as predictably, the press waded in. *The Times* took an especially lofty view. Forgetting how many of its readers bet on the horses without a second thought, it waxed lyrical on the morals of the affair. 'What of the purity of the sport?' it wailed. Other newspapers poured scorn on the scheme. 'Football Fixture Fiasco,' roared one; 'The Big Hush,' sniggered another, while a third, echoing the problem facing most genuine fans, simply printed the headline 'United v ???'. But the League would not give way.

The next Saturday attendances were down again. This time, some of the clubs sounded out the views of their supporters. At Hillsborough, a poll at the ground showed only 10% support for the League. At Elland Road the crowd roared out a lusty 'Yes' when asked over the Tannoy system if they wanted the old fixture list back. The pools companies seemed quite unaffected by it all. The volume of returns to them stayed at their usual levels and the only problem appeared to be that post offices were now inundated with purchases of postal orders on Saturday, rather than Friday, mornings. The ones facing the squeeze were not the pools companies but the soccer clubs, the very people the Football League existed to protect and encourage.

It was climb-down time and, to his credit, Charlie Sutcliffe clambered off his perch with dignity, grace and frankness. 'Whatever is thought necessary, whatever the clubs wish me to do, will be done.' He was a talented and devoted servant of football, who gave his life to the Football League. In all his years of work for it, this was the only occasion when he was proved to be wrong. In the years ahead, he never attempted to minimise the size of the clanger he dropped.

A Payne in the Butt

Luton Town v Bristol Rovers, 1936

History does not record whether Bristol Rovers were a touch demob-happy as they journeyed to Luton Town on Easter Monday at the back end of the 1936 season. We can be sure that Luton were not. They were still pushing for promotion from the Third Division (South). Rovers at least travelled hopefully, since they had held Luton 2–2 at home only three days earlier, so maybe they could pick up another point.

They would have been bucked on arrival to learn that none of Luton's three normal centre-forwards was fit to play and, in a fit of end-of-season expediency, one last opportunity in the No. 9 shirt was being given to a 22-year-old reserve wing-half who'd had only three outings in the first team. His name was Joe Payne, and, as he turned up at the ground to watch his mates play, he had no idea he'd be needed on the pitch. On hearing the news, the Bristol Rovers keeper probably looked forward to keeping a clean sheet. Little did he suspect that by the end of the afternoon he would be on the receiving end of history.

The first quarter of the game was uneventful. In bitterly cold rain and sleet, Payne had a miserable start, and was promptly dispossessed whenever the ball was played forward to him. But, after 23 minutes, a long punt upfield from the Luton goal found Payne, and Luton went one up. The two teams seemed evenly matched all the same, and it would have taken a brave soul to risk his money either way. But, five minutes before half-time, Luton scored again, this time through Roberts, and it was at this point that

Bristol Rovers abandoned the will to live. There were no visible signs of a collective suicide pact, only a complete inability to bottle up winger George Stephenson or to cut out the crosses that kept homing in on Payne. By half-time he'd completed his hat-trick and Luton were leading 4–0.

In the middle of the 1935–6 season, Bunny Bell of Tranmere had set a new individual scoring record with nine goals in the rout of Oldham Athletic by a score, 13–4, more reminiscent of a rugby match. In the Luton dressing room his teammates warned him he was in danger of beating the record, and no one took this light-hearted ribbing more seriously than Stephenson. Within twelve minutes of the restart, he had floated over three more crosses from the left for Payne to convert and, with a 7–0 deficit and half an hour still to go, Rovers were beginning to feel slightly silly.

But Joe Payne was just beginning to warm to his task. He'd already netted six with his boot and three with his head when Rovers more or less presented him with his tenth. He fell in the muddy goalmouth, the ball squirted in his direction, he swung a hopefully horizontal leg at it, and it bobbled apologetically over the line. What do you do when you are 11–0 down? In Rovers' case you give away a round dozen and George Martin helpfully rounded things up to a tidy 12–0.

Luton didn't make it to Division Two that year, but they did in 1936–7, and Joe Payne scored 55 of the goals that got them there. He also played once for England, and scored twice, but during Hitler's bid for promotion Payne suffered a couple of bad injuries. He was 32 when hostilities finished, and joined West Ham for a season. Compared with ten goals in ninety minutes, he could not be said to have taken centre stage, finishing with just four in the whole season. To this day, no other player has ever managed ten goals in an English league game.

Oh, I Do Love to Be Between the Uprights – Part One

Huddersfield v Barnsley, FA Cup, 1947; Manchester City v Preston, 1949

Goalkeepers are a law unto themselves, to which fundamental truth a number of clangers in this book pay eloquent testimony. Each generation likes to think that it has sole possession of the most cunning, devious or eccentric goalkeepers. In recent times Bruce Grobbelaar (see page 110) and David Seaman (see page 116) have dropped their fair share of clangers. No doubt a century ago the fans of Fatty Foulke (see page 11) swore there could never be another like him, and yet barely had he retired before Albert Iremonger was causing endless delight and frustration with Notts County and Lincoln City.

In his recent autobiography, Bob Wilson retold the story of Iremonger's celebrated penalty attempt. Bored with life on his own line, he thrust aside his eager colleagues and insisted on taking a spot kick his side had won, and as he had a hefty hoof they were willing to indulge him. He shivered the crossbar so forcefully that the ball rebounded almost to the centre circle. Albert set off in frantic pursuit of the bouncing sphere before the opposition could claim it, gave the ball a desperate toe poke as he caught up with it and watched helplessly as it flew straight as an arrow into his own net at the other end of the field. They just don't make 'em like that any more – or do they?

In an incident reminiscent of a spot of trouble England and Arsenal's David Seaman would suffer half a century later, the Huddersfield goalkeeper Bob Hesford was pottering around his area in the fading moments of his side's 1947 third-round Cup tie against Barnsley. The play was off in the distance, the score was 3–3 and a replay seemed inevitable. What Hesford failed to take into account was that the ball had arrived at the feet of the gifted and eccentric Jimmy Baxter.

Jimmy loved his football so well that he was prepared to put his packet of fags aside for two periods of 45 minutes every Saturday. As if that weren't sacrifice enough, he was playing on this particular day under the additional handicap, or so *The Times* reported, of a broken jaw encased in plaster. Looking up, he saw Hesford thirty yards or so in the distance, in the general area of the penalty spot and clearly contemplating the unfair vagaries of life. He flicked the ball into the air and volleyed it up, up, over and down into the goal behind Hesford. With that shot he won, said *The Times*, 'a noble victory'. For the young Michael Parkinson watching his hero, it was 'a goal of such wit and imagination' that he has never forgotten it. It's very unlikely Hesford ever forgot it either.

A couple of years later, the great Frank Swift of Manchester City and England was approaching the end of his distinguished career. Over time he had established a clear routine for the beginning of a game. He would carefully lay his cap flat in the back of the net, no doubt with an affectionate pat, before taking up his position on the line for battle to commence. (Most goalkeepers of the day wore flat caps – the hard peak could come in handy for dotting an opposing centre-forward on the bridge of the nose if he was challenging for a high ball.)

One unfortunate day in 1949, when City were playing Preston, the ref thoughtlessly blew his whistle to start the game before ascertaining that Frank was ready and comfortable. He was, in fact, still bending over with his back to the business of the day, attending to the needs of his cap, when, in a companionable kind of way, the ball joined him in the back of the net. Seeing him preoccupied with his pre-match rituals, Preston had essayed a speculative long shot and were rewarded with a new record for the fastest goal – seven seconds!

Oh, I Do Love to Be Between the Uprights – Part Two

The irrepressible Ugolini and others, 1940s and 1950s

Of course it's desperately unfair to single out goalkeepers as clanger droppers. After all, theirs may simply be the final act in a string of defensive weaknesses without which they might never have been forced into desperate error. But, then again, it's fun, and, since they get plenty of credit for spectacular last-ditch heroics, why not?

Bernard Stretton, all five foot eight of him, definitely fell into the spectacular category as he hurled himself around Luton Town's goalmouth (and England's on a day when Frank Swift was injured) in the late 1940s and 1950s. Bernard tended to celebrate a good save by swinging one-handed from the crossbar, though he generally managed to suppress the desire to thump himself on the chest with the other.

Then there was Ray Middleton of Chesterfield, a solid upright member of the community and a magistrate who dispensed justice from the bench on weekdays. Saturdays were a different matter, calling for authority of a more direct kind. By this stage, goalkeepers had acquired more rights to protection than they enjoyed in Fatty Foulke's day, but were not ring-fenced by legal niceties as they are today. They still had to guard against being bundled bodily into the net if they happened to be in contact with

41

the ball at the time. Middleton was fond of punching an airborne ball out of his area and, since big strikers were equally fond of heading the keeper into the net, he was reputed to have perfected a double-handed technique, reserving one fist for the ball and the other for the striker's head.

Rolando Ugolini of Middlesbrough came high on the list of unpredictable keepers off whom one never took one's eye for fear of missing something memorable. As you will by now have gathered, the perfect centre-forward of the postwar era was considered to have the build of a medium-sized tank. One such was Arsenal's Ronnie Rooke, who enhanced his menacing air with a chin that, in a men's outfitters, would have had an 'Extra Large' rating. In a Good Friday encounter at Highbury in the late 1940s, Ronnie was ambling back upfield while Ugolini prepared to take a goal kick. At the thud of leather on solid leather, Ronnie turned round, the ball hit him on the point of the chin with the velocity of an anti-aircraft shell and shot back past Ugolini into the empty net. One–nil to the Arsenal. It was the only goal Ronnie could never remember in later years. He was out cold.

Then there was the instance, fondly remembered by Michael Parkinson, when Middlesbrough met Sheffield Wednesday in the early 1950s. It was another of those days when Ugolini fell short of perfection in guarding his net. Wednesday were the proud possessors of their very own pocket battleship at centre-forward, by name Derek Dooley. In addition to being iron-clad, he had the virtue of being fast and was by nature possessive when it came to ownership of the ball. He saw no reason to take no for an answer. Against Boro, a well-timed pass split the defence for him to run onto. Ugolini set out to intercept it but, as he bore down on the ball, there passed though his mind a series of rapid equations on the odds against his getting there first, as well as on the size, weight, angle, trajectory and strike power of the guided missile called Dooley approaching fast from the opposite direction. Without stopping to check his calculations on the back of an envelope, he concluded it was a fifty–fifty venture. He stepped gallantly to one side and, like a matador sweeping his red cloak before the bull, ushered Dooley towards the empty net.

Hungarian Goulash – With Salt and Pepper

England v Hungary, 1953

Is it an English characteristic secretly to believe ourselves the best in the world, or is it one we share with every other country? In soccer terms, many English fans in November 1953 genuinely believed in their team's invincibility. England had never, in their whole footballing history, been beaten on their own soil, and barely any of the 100,000 who crowded into Wembley expected the match against Hungary, the reigning Olympic champions, to become a catalyst, a traumatic shock. 'We believed we were good at the game,' the England manager, Walter Winterbottom, said. 'Everybody expected us to win.' Not quite everybody.

The respected soccer writer Brian Glanville had watched Hungary trounce Italy 3–0 six months earlier and had described in *Sports Weekly* what might hit England if they did not urgently rethink their tactical approach – or indeed think about it at all. Two weeks before the Wembley game, Sweden fought out a 2–2 draw with Hungary under the management of George Raynor, a Yorkshireman whose astute tactical eye, ignored in his native land, kept Nandor Hidegkuti, the Hungarian playmaker, out of the game. Raynor went here, there and everywhere looking for talented players and, when he found them, he coached them in the style he wanted.

These were not things Winterbottom did or was encouraged to do by the FA, for whom the manager was there to do little more than give the lads a quick pep talk before the game began and make sure the bathwater was hot at the end of it. Raynor had instructed two of his players, a different one in each half, to mark Hidegkuti so tightly his face would turn red, and the ploy worked. By contrast, Winterbottom sought out Harry Johnston, England's centre-half, and politely asked if he felt in the mood for man-to-man marking or would rather stand off Hidegkuti. He stood off, and Hidegkuti had an afternoon to tell the grandchildren about.

Admittedly, it took him time to warm up. More than sixty seconds had gone before he had the first of his hat-trick in the back of the net as he stormed from his deep position onto a pass from Bozsik. Stan Mortensen equalised before Hidegkuti made it 2–1. In less than half an hour, it was 4–1. Stanley Matthews and Mortensen refused to give up and pulled back a goal before half-time, but, said Geoffrey Green in *The Times*, 'it could no more turn back the tide than if a fly had settled on the centre circle'.

The slaughter continued after half-time. Hidegkuti made it 6–2 with a perfect volley from a lobbed pass by Ferenc Puskas, the Galloping Major, and, although Alf Ramsey put away a consolation penalty, England had been taught a lesson. Hidegkuti 'played deep in the rear', wrote Green, 'supplying the link to probing and brilliant inside forwards and fast wingers, scoring three goals himself and leaving Johnston a lonely, detached figure on the edge of the penalty area.' Hungary played what came to be known as 4–2–4, familiar enough in the ensuing years, but revolutionary then. The England players simply didn't know whom they were supposed to be marking or necessarily where to find them if they did. The wingers would change wings from time to time, the full backs ran forward, overlapping their wingers while the inside-forwards dropped back into defence. This was all too much for simple English minds. The result was that while England had five shots on goal (scoring with three of them) Hungary had 35. It was hardly surprising that they were known as the Golden Team.

It took time for the lesson to sink in. Being beaten at home for the first time was mildly embarrassing to the powers-that-be but, with luck, it would be overlooked as a temporary aberration. When England played the return in Budapest, waved off with headlines such as that in the *Daily*

Express ('We'll blast the Magyars'), and this time were annihilated 7–1 it was another matter. The great Tom Finney was fit to play on this occasion, and he made clear his opinion. 'It brought home to English people that we were no longer the so-called best side in the world and hadn't been for some time. It was like carthorses playing racehorses.' Or, as centre-half Syd Owen said, 'like playing people from outer space'.

Things had to change. Dave Sexton, later an outstanding manager, was watching the football lesson at Wembley. 'We saw our game was static, but theirs was about passing and movement,' he said. It took time, but in the end clubs began to appoint coaches as well as managers, and actually produced a ball at training in order to learn a few basic skills.

Hungarian Goulash – With Sauerkraut

West Germany v Hungary, World Cup final, 1954

World Cup finals are always tense. National pride and honour is at stake, but this was something different. The Hungarians, the 'Golden Team', remembered what Nazi Germany had done in Hungary during World War II. What is more, when the two teams had met in a qualifying round the Germans had – so the Hungarians thought – set out cynically to maim their greatest star, Ferenc Puskas. Hungary routed their opponents 8–3, but Puskas had indeed been carried off seriously injured and it was touch and go whether he would recover for the final. He did, but there was more than just rivalry in the air. There was hatred and determination to win.

After their drubbing in the qualifying round, the Germans began to improve. Above all, they seemed to develop the stamina to keep going at full pace for the full ninety minutes. What, people began to ask behind their hands, were they taking? The final was played at the Wankdorf Stadium in Berne in pouring rain before 60,000 spectators who, despite the chaotic Swiss disorganisation, had somehow squeezed into their seats in time. With barely five minutes gone, the German goalkeeper, Turek, dropped the ball, and Puskas drove it into the net. Three minutes later, Turek dropped another clanger as he collided with one of his own players, and Czibor scored. But within ten more minutes the Germans had pulled both goals back. Both teams hammered away at top pace,

46

creating chances that went begging, and at half-time it was still 2–2. It was proving a final to remember.

At the start of the second half, the Hungarians metaphorically threw everything at the Germans in an effort to break both their goal line and their spirit. Not only did they have much to avenge, they also knew that failure, even by the 'Golden Team', was not tolerated in the communist state from which they came, nor by the Russian puppet master behind it. Turek had put his earlier mistakes to the back of his mind, and now played brilliantly, three times saving near-certain goals.

Bit by bit, Germany weathered the storm as, almost imperceptibly, the Hungarians began to tire on the sodden pitch. Even so, there was one last, golden chance to score the vital goal. With 78 minutes gone, Czibor let fly with a tremendous drive that not even the now-inspired Turek could hold. As it rebounded, it fell into the path of a striker as lethal as Puskas – Nandor Hidegkuti. He had the whole goal at his mercy. Ninety-nine times out of a hundred, he would have scored wearing a blindfold, but he stabbed at it and pushed it into the side netting. He sank to his knees as though he knew he'd lost the match.

Disheartened and tiring in the mud, the Hungarians were playing on their reserves of willpower. The Germans seemed unaffected, almost as fresh as when they had kicked off, and it was little surprise when, six minutes later, they scored. But Puskas was not a man to accept defeat. He went to each one of his players demanding one last push and, with three minutes remaining, a beautiful pass slid into his path in the German penalty area. With great precision, he placed the ball clear of Turek and into the net before vanishing from sight beneath a pile of relieved players and Hungarian officials.

But it was all in vain. The linesman's flag was up, and, although the English referee had at first given the goal, he reversed his decision and gave Germany a free kick for offside. Czibor had one last effort in the dying seconds, producing yet another glorious save from Turek, a villain who had turned into hero. Then it was all over. Germany had won 3–2, and the Hungarians wept.

In Budapest, riots broke out. Shops were looted, cars and trams were set alight. Military guards were placed outside players' homes, and their children were attacked on the way to school. Sackfuls of hate mail were delivered, to Puskas in particular. All for a game of soccer. Finally, the manager, Gustav Sebes, was sacked and the 'Golden Team' was broken up. Officially, it was stale.

Only a few months later, the whole of Hungary was ablaze, in revolt against the Russians, and the tanks began to roll onto the streets. But had this cataclysmic defeat been suffered on merit alone? Back in the 1950s the use of drugs was sometimes suspected, but testing facilities were many years into the future. Puskas had his own beliefs, and he showed no fear in voicing them. The West German changing rooms, he said, 'smelt like a garden of poppies. That is why they ran and chased like steam engines.' But there were few others who wished or dared to speak about it publicly.

And then, in the spring of 2004, the doubts that had been suppressed for half a century started rising to the surface in Germany in a book and two TV documentaries. The former groundsman at the Berne stadium claimed to have found used syringes under the drainage covers and to have been sworn to secrecy by a friend to whom he handed them. It was known that eight of the victorious team were taken seriously ill after the final. Three had jaundice and one had black fever, two died of cirrhosis of the liver (although one of them was a teetotaller), while the other two players' illnesses were not specified.

Professor Franz Loogen admitted to injecting the players but only, he said, with vitamin C, which, it was then believed by some, increased stamina. His fear was that the syringes might not have been properly sterilised beforehand. Hans Schafer, Germany's outside-left in the final, confirmed the players had been injected, but not with drugs. 'We were not doped, and I don't have a bad conscience,' he said.

It is a pity the truth may never be fully established. If there is no truth in the allegations, it leaves a very fine West German team with a slur upon their name. If the opposite was the case, it robbed the 'Golden Team' of the greatest honour they could have gained.

The Clown Prince Draws a Blank

Len Shackleton publishes his autobiography, 1956

Len Shackleton was one of soccer's great names in the 1940s and 1950s. After six years, and 166 goals, for Bradford Park Avenue he was transferred to mighty Sunderland at the beginning of 1948 for a then-record fee of £20,050, and played for them 348 times, scoring 101 goals. He would have won more England caps than he did but for stiff competition from players such as Wilf Mannion and Stan Mortensen, and the fact that his highly individualistic style caused many people to conclude he was not a team player.

However unfair that may have been, there was no doubting the pleasure he gave crowds everywhere, and not just the Roker Park faithful, with his unorthodox skills and flashes of humour. It has to be said, though, that some of his opponents did not always take kindly to being left with egg on their faces as he displayed his prodigious abilities at their expense. But the press loved it, and labelled him the 'Clown Prince of Soccer'.

Fifty years ago, soccer was still in the Dark Ages as far as the rights of players were concerned. Your club owned you and could dispose of you as and when it pleased, paying you in the meantime a sum of money for your services that in most cases barely kept your family's body and soul together. Shackleton played soccer because he loved it and was good at it, but he had his *amour propre*. His opinion of those who ran soccer was not high, and when his autobiography, *The Clown Prince of Soccer*, appeared in 1956, a year before injury forced his retirement, he made his views plain. On the opposite page is reproduced his chapter entitled 'The Average Director's Knowledge of Football'. What a fuss it caused! They were so cross with him, you'd have thought he'd run off with their daughters (he hadn't, as far as I know). But Len was Len and nearing the end of his career, and very, very slowly they smoothed down their ruffled feathers.

'The Average Director's Knowledge of Football',
a chapter from *The Clown Prince of Soccer*
by Len Shackleton (1956)

(The blank page summed up exactly what Shackleton thought of the average football director.)

A Clanger Ill-rewarded

Aston Villa v Manchester United,
FA Cup final, 1957

Defining a clanger can sometimes be tricky. Is an act of violence that completely changes the outcome of a game a clanger, even though unpremeditated? And what if that act gives victory to the side that committed it? McParland's charge on Ray Wood in the sixth minute of the 1957 Cup final is still debated by those old enough to remember it.

Matt Busby's Babes had already won the League title by the time they stepped onto the Wembley pitch for the final and, if they lifted the Cup, they would become the first team to do the double in the twentieth century, and the first since their opponents, Aston Villa, had achieved it in 1897. Cup finals seemed jinxed in the 1950s. Substitutes were not allowed back then, and both Arsenal in 1952 and Manchester City in 1955 lost after being reduced by injury to ten men.

In 1953, the Stanley Matthews final, Bolton went down at the last gasp carrying two wounded passengers, and in 1956 Manchester City's goalkeeper, Bert Trautman, had played with a broken neck, albeit on a winning side. Lightning was about to strike yet again. In a flight of prose of the deepest purple, *The Times* wrote, 'The imp that lives in the velvet turf has shown its spite to create unequal odds and spoil the occasion for the crowd.'

Because of the spate of injuries that had marred recent Cup finals, the FA had considered allowing an injured goalkeeper to be substituted, but had turned the idea down with only 24 hours to go before kick-off. In retrospect, perhaps this was the *real* clanger. Right from the start, Villa played what is sometimes called 'muscular football'. It seemed clear to the onlookers in the crowd and on television that their aim was literally to knock their formidable opponents out of their stride. 'Some of the challenges went beyond the bounds of respectability,' the press reported the following day.

Then, in the sixth minute, came the incident that ruined the game. United's goalkeeper, Ray Wood, saved a header from the Villa winger McParland, was charged by McParland and was badly hurt. He had a depressed fracture of the cheekbone, and was so badly dazed he left the field for an hour, returning in the second half to wander on the wing, still clearly away with the fairies. 'The way McParland accelerated over those last few strides to thunder into Wood seemed quite unnecessary,' said *The Times*, adding drily, 'No doubt it was not premeditated.'

If not premeditated then it was an ill-conceived and badly executed challenge, and therefore a clanger. But unlike most clangers, which end up penalising the side or the individual that dropped them, this one bounced back in Villa's favour to a degree that was unpalatable to all but the most partisan supporters. Jackie Blanchflower had to take over the goalkeeping duties and United's midfield, pulled out of shape as a result, was eliminated as the effective force it had been all season. Aston Villa scored twice in the second half and, with cruel irony, McParland got them both. United's ten men (or ten and a quarter with Wood now wandering up and down the wing in a semiconscious effort to draw a defender away from the centre) staged a surging rally towards the end in an attempt to snatch an improbable draw, and Tommy Taylor did get one in the net from a Duncan Edwards cross, but it was all too late. 'A heroic last effort brought a touch of grandeur to a bitter-sweet day,' said *The Times* – but Manchester had nothing else to show for it.

For Villa, it was a record-breaking seventh Cup final victory. It was also the third time Villa had used the final to see off pretenders to their unique record as the only holders of the double. In 1905 they had beaten Newcastle United, in 1913 Sunderland and now, whatever the means, Manchester United. As for United, they continued to thrill with their talented, exciting football for another nine months. Then came the tragedy of the Munich air crash, which cost so many of the Busby Babes their lives.

The Best-Loved Clanger of All Time

Juventus v Torino, 1957–8

When John Charles died in March 2004 he was mourned universally and from the heart. Not just in Wales, his country, or Leeds, his principal British club, but in Italy as well. He spent five years with Juventus as a goal scorer of unparalleled prowess, and within weeks became famous the length and breadth of the country.

'He had the features of Marlon Brando, the body of a light-heavyweight boxer, the breathing of a tiger and the bite of a snake,' said the *Gazzetta della Sport*. On one occasion he attended a star-strewn film premiere, and was astonished to hear the crowds calling not for Lollobrigida or Loren, but 'Giovanni, Giovanni' in an attempt to catch his attention. None of this turned his head or changed him in any way from what he always had been and always would be – *Il Buon Gigante*, the Gentle Giant.

It went without saying that a striker playing in Serie A – famous, or infamous, for its all-out defensive tactics – would be subjected to plenty of tough treatment, and the more goals John Charles scored and the more celebrated he became, the more determined the attention he received. Yet not once did he retaliate. He went through an entire footballing career without being sent off or receiving a single booking. Small wonder that in a recent poll he was voted Serie A's greatest foreign player of all time, and if you consider the many great names – including Maradona, Platini and countless Brazilian stars – who have plied their soccer skills in Italy this must rank as one of the greatest of accolades.

Yet he is remembered in Turin not just for his supreme skills but for one famous incident that epitomised John Charles. In the course of a local derby between Torino and Juventus in his first Italian season, he beat the opposing centre-half and had only the keeper to beat – and that was a confrontation that could only have one result. But, in his own words, as he told the press, 'I accidentally struck him [the centre-half] with my elbow and knocked him clean out. I only had the goalie to beat, but it didn't seem fair, so I kicked the ball out for a shy so the fella could have treatment.'

For a few moments the stadium went completely quiet. The Torino fans couldn't believe what they'd just seen, and the Juventus fans couldn't work out why he'd done it. In a modern context it would have driven the manager to the heights of profanity and would be condemned as almighty stupidity. It wasn't so very different in Serie A back in those days. But that wasn't the way it worked out.

Instead of abusing him, the crowd loved him for it. He had been admired and idolised before. Now he was loved, by Juventus and Torino fans alike. After another local derby between the two sides, he was catching up on some well-earned sleep at home when, 'I was woken up at about three in the morning by this incredible din of car horns. When I went out on the balcony there was a traffic jam of Torino fans hanging out of the windows waving their flags.'

Being the Gentle Giant, he invited them in, where they spent what was left of the night drinking his wine and trying to persuade him he'd be even happier playing for their team! His funeral service was held in St Peter-at-Leeds. The church was full way beyond overflowing and hundreds stood outside to pay their last respects. Among them were many Italians.

Reg Takes Leafe of Barcelona at Top Speed

Barcelona v Real Madrid, European Cup, 2nd round, 1960

If you're weary of life and seeking an original way to end it quickly, if not necessarily painlessly, this is what you do. Go to Madrid and stand outside Real's Bernabeu Stadium with a large placard saying 'I love Arthur Ellis and Reg Leafe'. Within five minutes you'll be enjoying eternal rest. If, on the other hand, it's free drinks you're after, take the same placard to the Nou Camp in Barcelona. Ellis and Leafe were the two English referees who took charge of the home and away legs of Real's second-round European Cup tie with Barcelona, and it would be fair to say that on each occasion half the crowd was a little displeased with their decisions.

The rivalry between the two clubs is legendary. It is also deep and bitter, fuelled, as it is, by the events of the Spanish Civil War and the period of Fascism that followed under Franco. The Catalans of Barcelona saw themselves as victims and, since Real was Franco's favoured team, the hatred fell easily into place. It did not help, of course, that from 1956 to 1960 Real won the European Cup, and with it undying glory, for five years in succession. Nevertheless, the feeling was abroad, and with some justification, that the great team had breasted the summit of the hill and were beginning to descend the other side. The European Cup campaign of 1960–1 might, just might, be Barca's turn.

The first leg was in Madrid. It was a tight and gripping encounter that seemed set to end at 2–1 in favour of Real, a score for which Barcelona might well have settled in advance with the home leg still to come. As full time approached, a beautiful through ball split the Real defence and fell at the feet of the great Hungarian, Sandor Kocsis. The linesman's flag went up, apparently for offside, but Arthur Ellis waved play on. Just inside the box, Kocsis was unceremoniously floored, and Ellis signalled a penalty. It needs little imagination to envisage the pandemonium that followed. Obviously he was offside. Clearly he dived. Who's paying whom and why? And so on and so forth. Ellis was unmoved, the penalty was taken and scored, and to say that the city of Barcelona erupted in joy would be an understatement.

A fortnight later, another English referee, Reg Leafe, took charge of the return. 'This is the game of all time,' said Kenneth Wolstenholme, reporting for the BBC. 'Real were held on their own ground to a 2–2 draw, so they are really up against it tonight in Barcelona.' And indeed they were. Up against not just Barcelona but every Catalan that breathed and, as it transpired, up against Mr Leafe as well. Even Santiago Bernabeu himself, though a great advocate of remaining dignified in all circumstances, later permitted himself the brief remark that 'Mr Leafe had been Barcelona's best player.'

Controversy soon raged on both sides as each had an early goal disallowed. Then a Barcelona shot took a big deflection off a Real defender and trickled over the line as goalkeeper Vicente looked on, wrong-footed. Real stormed forward desperately. Twice they had the ball in the back of the net and each time Reg Leafe, who seemed to many impartial observers to be out of his depth in the intimidating atmosphere, disallowed the goals. Nine minutes from full time, the issue was effectively settled as Barca caught Real on the break, sped to the goal line and crossed for Evaristo to head past Vicente.

Real refused to give up, but although they snatched one back they could not force another and, for the first time in their history, they were out of the European Cup. Five times Real had had the ball in the net, only for Mr Leafe to rule out four of their attempts. Phil Ball, the historian of Real's first hundred years, has looked at the old black-and-white film of the game. 'It has to be said', he writes, 'that Madrid's protests had some substance. None of them [the "goals"] appears in any way illegal.'

Within minutes of the game's end, infuriated Real supporters were rumoured to be hunting Mr Leafe, and it was not his hand they wanted to shake. He was hurried through a side exit and thrown into a taxi hastily procured by a British journalist. Of one thing one can be reasonably sure: he did not thereafter take his holidays in Spain. That same evening Kenneth Wolstenholme had declared that 'everybody believes that whoever wins tonight will win the European Cup'. To the unrestrained joy of the Madrilenos, he was wrong. In the final Barcelona were beaten 3–2 by Benfica, the emerging stars who were to assume Real's mantle.

Spurs Whistled Out of the Eagles' Eyrie

Benfica v Tottenham Hotspur, European Cup semi-final, Lisbon, 1962

An eagle's nest is its eyrie, a formidable fortress that no sane raider approaches. Benfica were the Eagles, Lisbon's Stadium of Light was their eyrie, the first half of the 1960s were their greatest years, and Spurs were the intrepid raiders. Benfica were led by the astounding Black Panther, Eusebio, supported by Coluna and Jose Augusto; Spurs were led by a genius called Jimmy Greaves, supported by Danny Blanchflower and Dave McKay.

Spurs were unquestionably the best and most attractive team in England at the time and this semi-final was, to all intents and purposes, the European Cup final. To be sure, Real Madrid were already through to the final, but their ageing team could no longer claim to be Europe's finest.

Playing to the instructions of their manager, Bela Guttman, the Eagles began like an electric storm. For twenty minutes Spurs struggled to contain them as goals from Aguas and Jose Augusto gave them a 2–0 lead. But Spurs were much more than just a pretty side whose crisp, first-time passing dazzled spectators. They were also a team of fight and determination. Slowly and steadily, they damped the forest fire and pressed forward themselves. Early in the second half Bobby Smith, their rampaging centre-forward with the build of a barrel on legs but the pounce of a tiger, scored to make it 2–1. David Mellet, the Swiss referee, scratched his head and tried to think of a reason to disallow it, but couldn't.

Minutes later, Spurs had the ball in the net again. This was the cue for Herr Mellet to spring to life like a cuckoo from a cuckoo clock. Offside, he opined. Impossible, said almost everyone else, especially those who had crossed the Channel. Greavesie had carried the ball up to and round the full back before scoring. Not much longer had passed before Bobby Smith had the ball in the net for his second of the game. First, Herr Mellet signalled a goal, then thought of something that made sense to him, at least, recanted and signalled a free kick for offside. Once again, no one could see who or why. Greaves had taken the ball through the Benfica defence, all shipshape and Bristol fashion, before pulling the ball back for Smith to hammer into the net. The law that deemed such a move offside simply didn't exist. Worse was to follow. Almost immediately, Benfica hared off up the pitch and Jose Augusto headed a third goal for Benfica. Instead of winning 3–2 or, at worst, drawing 3–3 with three away goals safely in the bank, Spurs were as good as out of the European Cup. It was enough to make you slap an embargo on Swiss watches.

The return at White Hart Lane was a humdinger, one of the best and most exciting games to be played on British soil. There was only one tactic Spurs could pursue, and that was all-out attack. Time and again, it left them wide open at the back and, after fifteen minutes, Simoes scored an away goal to make it 4–1 on aggregate. Spurs had not come this far for nothing, and wave after attacking wave washed over Benfica's defence.

Spurs and Greavesie had yet another goal disallowed, but still they drove forward. Bobby Smith scored shortly before half-time, Danny Blanchflower from the penalty spot soon after, and three times Spurs crashed the ball against crossbar and uprights, but the third goal just would not come. Spurs won the home leg 2–1, but lost 3–4 on aggregate. At the final whistle, the crowd that had booed Benfica onto the pitch gave both teams a standing ovation but, in their hearts, they knew those two astonishing refereeing decisions in Lisbon had been the vital difference between meeting Real Madrid in the final, and crashing out of the competition. Benfica duly beat Real Madrid 5–3 to lift the European Cup for the second consecutive year and, in 1963, Spurs won the European Cup Winners' Cup.

The Tarnishing of a Good Player

Argentina v England, World Cup quarter-final, 1966

To any Englishman old enough to remember the World Cup quarter-final clash (the word is carefully chosen) between Argentina and England at Wembley in 1966, the performance of the former's captain, Antonio Rattin, is an unforgettable disgrace. There is no avoiding the fact that it was. Yet one can only regret that a fine, creative player is remembered, in Europe at least, only for violence and skulduggery when, but for third-party instructions, he and his side might have been left to play the skilful and captivating game of which they were more than capable.

Just where the third-party instructions began their journey can only be surmised, given how politicised soccer usually is in Latin America, but their eventual mouthpiece was the manager of the national side, Juan Lorenzo. The instructions he gave Rattin and his team were to avoid defeat at any cost and using any tactics, and if that meant a goalless draw and the spin of a coin to decide who progressed to the semi-finals, so be it. If the coin came down the wrong way at least back home the blame for defeat could be attributed to fate. Fortunately for England the referee was a tough German of unyielding character who refused to be cowed by even the most intimidating of challenges.

Within a matter of minutes of the ferocious start Rattin was booked, and within half an hour four more Argentine players had been warned as to their future behaviour. Almost every free kick against Argentina saw Rattin locked nose to nose in angry disputation with the referee, while tackles were flying in with the freedom of a saloon brawl in a Hollywood Western. After 35 minutes, the referee's temper finally gave way as Rattin spat at him following another decision against his side. He was immediately sent off.

The order was one thing, its execution quite another. Rattin refused to go, the team jostled round the referee, where they were joined by sundry Argentine officials, and the quarter-final came to a complete halt. It was only when FIFA themselves sent someone down to tell Rattin that he either departed forthwith or Argentina would be expelled from the Cup immediately that he finally agreed to be escorted to the dressing room. Two policemen accompanied him with stately tread to ensure he didn't make a bolt for it and return to the fray. Unfortunately for Rattin, he had exited stage left, furthest from the tunnel, instead of stage right, and on his long progression around the pitch insults, and other gestures requiring little description but not calculated to improve the atmosphere, were exchanged with the crowd.

The second half was fought out in much the same vein, and England only once, late in the day, managed to get through the ten-man Argentine defence to take the match 1–0. Behind the scenes after the game the general madness continued, or so it was reported, with Argentine players urinating in the tunnel, smashing a glass door and challenging the England players to switch from round ball to fisticuffs – an invitation they might well have taken up but for the risk that the tea might go cold.

If the instructions of the manager, Juan Lorenzo, had been stupid in the first place, the England manager, Alf Ramsey, made a remark of equal foolishness after the game when he informed the assembled press that the Argentines were 'animals'. He was tight-lipped with anger, and in all probability a great many English supporters would have been tempted to say the same or worse. Nevertheless, it was a gaffe the consequences of which are still with us. Add in the Falkland Islands (the Malvinas), not to mention Maradona and the infamous 'hand of God', and it's little wonder that, whenever Argentina and England meet these days, the tensions are high. So hands up those who thought soccer was just a game.

Catenaccio Murdered – Millions Celebrate

Celtic v Inter Milan, European Cup final, 1967

Inter Milan were champions of Europe three times in the four years from 1963 to 1966, and in that time had experienced defeat in Continental competitions just once. Their success was based on the formidable *catenaccio* defensive system. The word comes from the colloquial Italian for 'doorbolt', and crudely translated, this system entailed locking eleven men in and around your penalty area, grabbing just one goal on the break if you could, and strangling the life out of the game as a spectacle. Italians were its principal practitioners and high priests and, despised as it was the length and breadth of the footballing world, it worked, for a few years at least.

In the 1967 European Cup final, to which Inter Milan had once again progressed as though by divine right, they were pitched against Celtic. In the heat and humidity of Lisbon, the team from the cold north couldn't hope to play their normal game of constant movement and attack and last the pace for ninety minutes. Could they?

On the eve of the final Celtic's manager, the great Jock Stein, made a simple statement: 'Win or lose, we want to make the game worth remembering. We want to win playing good football.' From that moment there were no neutrals. Unless they were Italian, people everywhere were behind Celtic, but the start could not have been worse.

After only seven minutes, Craig upended Cappellini in the penalty area, and Mazzola gave Inter just the start they wanted from the spot. The eleven-man defence locked into place with a clang. Celtic did not seem to turn a hair. They had given a hint of what they intended in the very first minute of the match as Jimmy Johnstone on the right wing beat Burgnich, his marker, four times in a single confrontation. Keeping the ball virtually on his toecaps, he had beaten him on the outside, then the inside, outside again and, for good measure, the inside once again.

Nominally, Celtic were playing 4–2–4, but Tommy Gemmell on the left and Jim Craig on the right repeatedly swept forward in attack, overlapping their front four. Jock Stein had said 'I have the players trained to thinking the game, and they can work out things for themselves.' *Catenaccio* had never before encountered a game plan like this, put into operation by men with the wit and intelligence to adapt continuously. Its players were so bereft of creative instinct and, as Stein had gambled all along, so unaccustomed to thinking for themselves, that it had no answer. For four-fifths of the game, it was all Celtic going forward. 'Surge after surge of attacks beat down a defence like waves crashing against a rock,' wrote Geoffrey Green, doyen of soccer correspondents. But for Inter's outstanding goalkeeper, Giuliano Sarti, the final might well have become a rout. He pulled off save after astonishing save, some almost defying belief. Betweentimes, both Bertie Auld and Gemmell hit the post with Sarti beaten once just before and once just after the interval.

Sarti apart, Inter increasingly looked like a side destined to lose, 'a side without heart or skill, filled with apprehension', as Green said. As the second half progressed in the searing heat it was not the team from the cold north that was wilting. Instead, Inter's trainer patrolled the touchline, throwing buckets of cold water over the Latin players from the south. The inevitable equaliser came in the sixtieth minute as Gemmell lashed an unstoppable drive into the top of the net, but long before then 'Inter looked ravaged and unlovely'.

Cheered to the roof beams by the Portuguese crowd, as well as by their own delighted fans, the green and white hoops of Celtic continued to sweep ever forward. Inter had nothing to offer. They had relied on creating an impregnable cage around their penalty area, only to see Johnstone, Gemmell, Craig, Auld, Billie McNeill and the rest pick the locks repeatedly. It was a cowardly and unattractive way of playing 'the beautiful game', and now the price was being paid. Gemmell hit the bar, and somehow Sarti still found the spirit and courage to pull off wonderful saves to keep his otherwise dispirited team in with a chance of holding out, at least into extra time.

Seven minutes were left when the elastic of Inter's knickers finally snapped. Gemmell laid the ball off to Bobby Murdoch who shot, and saw the ball deflected by Steve Chalmers past Sarti. Almost nobody could bear to watch the last tense moments, but they need not have worried. Inter were spent and *catenaccio* was not only dead – one might almost call it suicide – but buried. The final whistle blew and the National Stadium became a scene of happy chaos as Scottish and Portuguese fans alike turned it into a party arena to celebrate the triumph of football.

When Things Go Pear-Shaped

Manchester City have a few problems, 1968

Manchester City looked a pretty fair side in 1967. Their management team of Joe Mercer and the colourful Malcolm Allison pulled off what proved to be a masterstroke by bringing in Francis Lee to join Mike Summerbee in the attack. City enjoyed a winning run of ten games and, as the year-end approached, found themselves second in the old First Division, buoyed by the self-confidence such success engenders.

On Boxing Day 1967, they were away to West Brom at the Hawthorns, confident of another victory. It was a tougher game than they anticipated and they went 2–0 down, but fought back to level the scores and were pressing for the winner when, without warning, the goalposts collapsed. That was the moment things began to go wrong. Declining to put down a couple of rolled-up jackets for a goal, despite there being only moments left for play, officialdom insisted the thing be done properly. When, after a lengthy delay, play restarted, City seemed to have lost the plot, and conceded a last-minute goal and two points. Four days later, they met WBA again in the return league fixture at Maine Road, lost that, and prepared for their home tie with Third Division Reading in the third round of the FA Cup on 3 January.

It turned out to be one of those games you wished you'd never forked out good money to watch. In a word, boring. No goals, no memorable moments and not a lot of skill – the kind of day the side in the higher division just hopes to get away with and out of its system. With a quarter of an hour to go, it looked as if City's prayers, limited though they had become by that point, were answered when they were awarded a penalty. Francis Lee stepped up to take it. He placed the ball carefully, concentrating on where to hit it. 'Right, I'm going to knock this to the keeper's left,' he decided. He was not a man to miss. Suddenly, as he walked back to begin his run-up, there was a noise as of a mighty rushing wind, and he was passed at speed by team-mate Tommy Coleman. No matter what side they support, every fan knows the player who once scored with a long-range drive and spends the rest of his career rocketing the ball twenty feet over the crossbar from every conceivable angle and distance. Coleman obviously belonged to that club. He charged up to the ball and smashed it high, wide and handsome into the crowd. Lee's language on the subject of what on earth he thought he was doing was colourful and even, by his own admission, forceful, but Coleman was cheerfully unabashed. 'I just fancied it,' he said.

That was as close to a goal as the long-suffering fans got. The replay at Reading's ground was a different matter altogether. City were dazzling, and won 7–0. As the final whistle went, the Tannoy crackled into life. 'Ladies and gentlemen,' said a disembodied voice, 'you have just seen one of the greatest teams England has ever produced.' Inevitably, therefore, City were knocked out in the next round.

The Miss of This or Any Other Year

Benfica v Manchester United, European Cup final, 1968

The first half of an emotional final at Wembley in 1968 was, said Geoffrey Green, nothing but 'busy dullness'. Ruthless Benfica tackling and 'a symphony of whistling from the referee broke the match in a thousand pieces'. It was an emotional evening because all the world that wasn't Portuguese was willing Matt Busby, and the Manchester United team he had recreated from the wreckage of Munich exactly ten years earlier, to win the European Cup. On the evidence of the first half it was going to be an uphill struggle, and the second half bore it out.

Bobby Charlton headed United into the lead, but either side of his goal two yawning opportunities went begging. Sadler, put clean through by Brian Kidd, missed the easiest of goals. It was, someone said, 'equivalent to dropping Sobers in the slips'. Later, after United had taken their 1–0 lead, George Best opened up the Benfica defence and shot with such power that goalkeeper Henrique could only parry the ball away, almost to the feet of Sadler who, in the favoured language of local reporters, again 'failed to convert'.

Despite United's period of dominance, it was not one-way traffic. According to Geoffrey Green, the celebrated 'Black Panther', Eusebio, whose fame was as far-flung as Charlton's, 'was constantly prowling like a caged, hungry animal'. Ten minutes into the second half, he had rocked

Alex Stepney's crossbar with a thunderbolt from twenty metres. Nobby Stiles was shadowing him everywhere, policing him as he had done during England's match with Portugal in the 1966 World Cup, but he needed to break free only once.

As the game entered its last fifteen minutes, United began visibly to tire and, on eighty minutes, Benfica scored, not through Eusebio but Graca, to make it 1–1. United were hanging on by their fingertips. It was Stiles who kept his teammates going, exhorting them and making jokes to keep their spirits up. Eusebio and Benfica pressed forward, desperate to settle matters within the ninety minutes, and then, with three minutes remaining, Eusebio broke clean through like the proverbial knife through butter. From almost point-blank range the deadly finisher shot – and Stepney, parrying it, pulled off not one, but two quite brilliant reflex saves. Not for a second should United's goalkeeper be denied every ounce of credit for his stunning performance, and yet how could Eusebio, of all people, be given two chances to win the Cup for Benfica and fail to take either of them?

It went to extra time, and in seven dramatic minutes of the first period United scored not once, not twice but three times to win the European Cup, the first English club to do so. 'They came back with all their hearts to show everyone what Manchester United is made of,' said Matt Busby afterwards. Jack Crompton, the trainer, showing marvellous sang froid once the final whistle had safely blown, agreed. 'We went out a bit towards the end of the second half,' he said with deadpan understatement, 'but then came back wonderfully.' Benfica, twice former winners, never lifted the European Cup again.

Thus Sprake the Lord

Chelsea v Leeds United,
FA Cup final, 1970

The Lord Sprake unto Gary and said, Thou shalt be an outstanding goalkeeper, and shalt win numerous caps, 37 to be precise, for – let me see, where will there be a vacancy? – Wales. But, in return for this great gift, thou shalt cause thy fellow men to guffaw mightily (except those of them that dwell in Leeds) with various mistakes that I shall visit upon thee when thou least expectest them. And so it came to pass, mostly in Cup ties.

The best of them has already been referred to in the Foreword. It happened at Anfield in a Cup replay. Jack Charlton hit a firm back pass to Sprake in the Leeds goal, turned to move upfield and heard a roar from the crowd. Oh no, he thought to himself, I hit it too hard. But he hadn't. Gary had gathered it safely, pivoted to throw out one-handed, forgotten to let go and, to the startled joy of the Kop, hurled it with malice aforethought into his own net. It is said they played the tune 'Careless Hands' over the Tannoy system as the crowd left the ground that day.

If Anfield was a pretty public stage on which to commit a howler, Wembley was an even bigger one. Leeds had never won the FA Cup, but they were at the zenith of their great, Don Revie-inspired days and had every reason to suppose they would break their duck against Chelsea in 1970.

The Wembley pitch was not in good shape for the match, patchy and wet, with sanded areas, and this helped materially with Leeds's opening goal after fifteen minutes. With Peter Bonetti out of position and McCreadie and Harris guarding the goal line, Jack Charlton headed downward from six yards out. McCreadie kicked the spot where he expected the ball to bounce, but it didn't, it crept furtively under his foot and over the line. Then, just before half-time, Sprake struck – or rather, failed to. Out on the left, Peter Houseman gathered a lobbed pass from McCreadie and essayed a weak, tentative poke in the general direction of the goal.

The great and glorious Gary had only to fall on it to gather. He fell most satisfactorily – indeed one might almost have said gracefully – but evidently forgot the reason he had adopted the prone position. The ball passed apologetically between his flailing arms and Houseman was gratified, if surprised, to find himself added to the list of those who have scored at Wembley. Leeds regained the lead with six minutes left but Chelsea, whose play throughout had refused to admit the possibility of defeat, snatched an equaliser in the 88th minute and went on to win the replay at Old Trafford 2–1.

The Most Deplorable Scenes

Leeds United v West Bromwich Albion, Elland Road, 1971

I know it all happened a third of a century ago but, even so, if you happen to be down Leeds way, best not to mention the name Ray Tinkler in polite conversation. But for Mr Tinkler, Leeds might have been flying the 1970–1 championship pennant. As it was, his decision making on that fateful day, 17 April, was enough to make Gary Sprake hurl the ball into his own net in disgust.

West Brom were the visitors to Elland Road that day and they hadn't won a game away from the Hawthorns for sixteen months. Leeds, on the other hand, were heading the table as the season came to its conclusion, even though the steady erosion of their earlier seven-point lead had allowed Arsenal to close the gap – almost. But the visit of West Brom promised two easy points and a chance, at worst, to hold their slender lead.

Unfortunately, the script was mislaid somewhere between Birmingham and Leeds because, midway through the second half, West Brom were clinging tenuously to a 1–0 lead. With twenty minutes gone in the second period, Tony Brown blocked an attempted pass by Norman 'bites yer legs' Hunter, and followed it up as it rebounded into the Leeds half. Meanwhile, West Brom's Colin Suggett was having a bit of a blow on the Leeds side of the centre circle, but was innocent of the ball as events unfolded. It was Jeff Astle who came racing up in support of Brown,

75

gathered his pass and thumped it uncompromisingly into the back of the net. The linesman had his flag up, though, for offside against Suggett, and the Leeds fans breathed a momentary sigh of relief until they realised Mr Tinkler was pointing to the centre circle. In his opinion Suggett, loitering in an offside position though he may have been, was doing so without intent and therefore could not be convicted of interfering with play. The goal stood. Two–nil to West Brom and 25 minutes left to play.

First, the Leeds players besieged the ref. Then a posse of Leeds fans, thirty or forty of them, invaded the pitch intent on discussing the finer points of the matter with him, and the Leeds players had to undergo a hurried conversion to guardians of the peace and protectors of officialdom. A stone came out of the crowd and scored a bull's-eye on the linesman's head. He retired nursing two headaches – one from the blow, the other from the effort of working out why he had been winged when he'd had his flag up all along. The law appeared with more sprightly tread than in the days of Charlie Sutcliffe (see page 9), and after five minutes and several arrests managed to restore order.

The press was predictably outraged by the scenes at Elland Road. 'Leeds appear to believe they have a divine right to win,' thundered the *Telegraph*, 'and they have an appalling habit of whingeing on and off the field if a decision goes against them.' There was some truth in the charge back in the 1970s, though judging from the comments of some of today's better-known Premiership managers the same accusations could still be made in certain quarters.

Leeds scored a late goal, but went down 2–1. Their defeat meant that Arsenal would be champions if they took both points from their last game of the season – against their north London rivals, Tottenham, at White Hart Lane. They left it late. Not until the eightieth minute could they score the goal they needed, but score it they did to snatch the championship from under Leeds's noses by a single point.

Getting the Best of Banks and Jennings

Northern Ireland v England;
Tottenham Hotspur v Manchester United, 1971

'Northern Ireland have never had a player remotely as good as Best in my time,' said fellow international and Spurs goalkeeper, Pat Jennings. Nor, for that matter, did anyone else in the world. 'El Beatle', as he was often known, was *the* player of the late 1960s and early 1970s. Ball skills, control on the ground and in the air, speed, shooting power with either foot, commitment and ambition – he had the lot, and plenty of other tricks to go with them. Jennings was happy to concede that Northern Ireland's chances of winning often depended on whether or not Best was playing.

In 1971 there was still an annual home international series in which England, Northern Ireland, Scotland and Wales all played each other. That year, Northern Ireland's game with England was in Belfast, and on the evidence of the play the home side was unquestionably the better. Nevertheless, they were 1–0 down when the great Gordon Banks gathered the ball as George Best followed up and danced attendance on him while he manoeuvred around his area preparing to kick downfield.

Finally, Banks threw the ball up to punt and, with lightning speed, Best's left foot hooked the ball away as it travelled the eighteen-odd inches from hand to foot, controlled it and rolled it into the net. He had not made any contact with Banks. Not so much as a hair of his manly head was ruffled. But, for whatever series of complex equations and half-remembered

77

rules, the referee disallowed the goal despite the understandable protests of the entire Northern Ireland team. There was no further score, and England were lucky to come away with a win.

Despite being ninety yards downfield, Pat Jennings had seen exactly what had happened. He was, in addition, one of Best's closest pals and they roomed together for away games, so one might have thought he would be prepared for what occurred a fortnight later when they met on opposite sides in a league game between Spurs and Manchester United. But he wasn't.

The scenario was similar to the one in Belfast. Jennings had gathered in his area, Best had followed through and was now loitering with intent. Jennings threw the ball up, preparing to hoof it a mile downfield, round came Best's foot, Jennings checked for a split second, not wishing to break his pal's leg as he went through with the kick, and before he knew it the ball was in the back of the net. But this time there was no referee to come to the rescue. Seeing the ball safely in the keeper's hands, the referee and the linesmen were all running back upfield, backs to the goal, ready for the ball to land like a howitzer in the other half of the pitch. Admittedly the ref looked bemused when he turned to see the ball in the last place he'd expected it but, as neither he nor the linesmen had been in a position to gather the evidence, sift it and reach a weighty judicial verdict, what could he do? One–nil to Manchester United and a very red-faced Pat Jennings!

Sod's Law

Manchester United v Manchester City, 1974

Clangers come in all sorts of guises. Some resound like Big Ben, some are barely audible, but the one Manchester United dropped in their 1974 relegation derby with City rang mournfully, like a muffled bell. Nobody, not even its villain – or was he the hero? – had the heart to think of it.

In 1960, Manchester City paid the then record transfer fee of £55,000 for a teenage Scot so gifted he would become known as 'the King': Denis Law. In the years that followed he cast a long shadow over football in Manchester, even though he left City in 1961 to become one of the first British players to go to Italy, spending a season with Torino. When he returned, once again breaking the transfer fee record with the first six-figure sum, it was to United, and it was with them that his great reputation was established. Between 1960 and 1974 he appeared in fourteen derbies between City and United – three for City and eleven for United. It was his last that would leave an indelible mark on the psyches of both teams.

By 1973, Law was past his best and no longer featured as an automatic choice for United. He reckoned, though, that he had one more season of skill and desire left in him so, out of the goodness of their hearts, United set him free to enjoy a last fling with his first Manchester club, City. They lived to regret it as they came to their penultimate game of the season, a local derby against City, needing a win to avoid relegation from the First Division. It was, or should have been, a possibility. They were at home, and City were in little better shape than they were, only six points ahead in the table.

Fifty-seven thousand packed into Old Trafford to see a relatively subdued and colourless game. United's midfield ensured they spent much of the game on the attack, but there was no striker, no Denis Law, to turn possession into goals. Twice they beat Joe Corrigan in the City goal, but both times their efforts were cleared off the line.

Then the near-inevitable happened. With four minutes left, Law found himself on the six-yard line, back to the United goal and with a defender closing in. An apologetic backward flick of his heel and the ball was in the net. It was the last time he touched the ball as a Manchester footballer. He walked away with an air of sadness and, as United fans invaded the pitch, he was substituted. The teams were taken off and not even Matt Busby's appeal could restore either Law or order. The referee declared the match finished after 86 minutes, and Denis was left with a very bittersweet memory to take into retirement.

Trust Me, All That Sand Down There's a Bunker

The confusing times of Don Revie, 1974–7

Picture the scene: date – 22 September, 1974; venue – Piccadilly Hotel, Manchester. A stream of fit-looking young men enter the doors. 'Which way to the England squad session?' 'Ah, yes, sir. Straight on and left at the end.' But, as more and more of them swarm in, the receptionist's face settles into a worried frown. Do they mean the England *football* squad or has there been a mistake in the booking? Perhaps it's the British Olympic squad having an early get-together for the 1976 games – in which case should we have reserved the conference centre?

But no. After 85 of them – that's nearly eight teams full, a thought Tony Hancock would have enjoyed – have crammed into the room, the doors are shut. Don Revie, newly appointed to succeed the great Alf Ramsey as England manager, rises to his feet and informs the startled multitude that 'Football is not an eleven-man game.' To be sure, he fell short of announcing a new FIFA initiative to play 85-a-side matches, but he had summoned quite a few players who had difficulty holding down a place in their club sides and who would never get within sniffing distance of an England cap. Among other ideas he floated was that win bonuses should be introduced, a thought that offended many present who believed playing for one's country was more than sufficient incentive.

The affair typified the inconsistencies that bedevilled Revie's actions. He seemed to have an unhealthy interest in money – there were indeed one or two respected players of the day who always insisted Revie had tried to bribe them to throw matches. Yet at the same time he believed the way to success was to recreate with England the club atmosphere that had brought him such success at Leeds between 1961 and 1974. The big difference was that at international level the time available to spend with the squad was limited to a few days now and again. Alf Ramsey overcame the problem by being consistent in selection and backing his boys even through occasional lapses in form. Revie went to the opposite extreme, changing captains and players apparently at random. 'You never felt you were number-one choice,' said Trevor Brooking. 'It unsettles you.'

The outcome, quite apart from constantly changing teams, often without a tactical plan, was a series of erratic results, with more gaffes than triumphs. Crisis loomed as England went into the World Cup qualifying matches of 1976. England's group contained Finland, Italy and Luxembourg, with only one winning through to the 1978 Cup proper. For the game in Rome against Italy, Revie picked a defensive team with one striker, QPR's Stan Bowles.

'It was the worst line-up Revie ever picked,' thought Mick Channon, a well-known England forward of the time. Maybe he expected the renowned Italian defensive blanket to be so nonplussed by a single striker that they'd somehow forget he was there. They didn't, and England lost 2–0. They failed to qualify for the World Cup, and followed up in 1977 by losing home friendlies in quick succession to Scotland, Wales and Holland.

Thoughts were then free to turn towards a three-match tour of South America fixed for the summer. Just before the first match, against Brazil, the squad was perplexed to learn that Revie would miss the game because he'd be watching Italy play Finland, a game now meaningless since England had failed their World Cup qualification. He turned up later, in time to take credit for draws against Argentina and Uruguay, and to suggest to the FA officials travelling with England that they might like to pay him in advance for the remaining eighteen months of his contract.

Not surprisingly, nobody other than Revie could see the advantage of this. Thereupon, he flew by roundabout routes to Dubai and signed a contract to manage their soccer team in return for lots of tax-free money. Negotiations were so secret that he took only one journalist with him (who had been expecting to accompany Revie to the Open Golf Championship in Scotland, but instead landed the biggest scoop of his life for himself and his paper, the *Daily Mail* no less).

In 1977 the tabloid press (of which, believe it or not, the *Mail* was not then a paid-up member) was less vicious and unreasoning towards soccer managers than it later became. Even so, opprobrium poured over Revie's absent head. He was the first person charged by the FA with bringing the game into disrepute, and the *Mirror* began to probe allegations of match fixing. Not until 1984 did he risk returning permanently to Britain. Still, some forgave him. Kevin Keegan, who had suffered from his managerial inconsistencies, reckoned that 'many of his faults were good qualities carried to extremes'. Answers on a postcard please, but not to this address.

Ole, Ola, Ole, Ola!

Ally McLeod and Scotland's World Cup, 1978

Once upon a time, in a land of mountains and lochs, there lived a wizard called Ally, Ally McLeod. He lived in a castle called Pittodrie, and spent all his time thinking of magic spells to win pots made of silver and gold. He had a football team called Aberdeen, and one day he tried out a new spell on them. There was a puff of smoke and a flash of lightning and there, before his very eyes, stood a big silver pot called the Scottish Cup. Everybody cheered and told him he was the best magician ever, or at least since the Big Jock himself, Wizard Stein.

A long way away, in a fairyland called Argentina, there was a golden cup called the Jules Rimet Trophy. It wasn't very big. You could pick it up in one hand and wave it about. But if you could get it you could have anything you liked for four years. Everybody wanted it. All the wizards in the world who had football teams went around trying out their magic spells on each other to see which ones would be allowed to go to Argentina to try to win the little gold cup. Next door to the Scottish lived a bad wizard called Revie, who had a team of wicked gnomes that was called England. The Scottish chortled like anything when Wizard Revie's spells turned out to be worse than useless and he went off in a sulk to live by himself in the desert (see page 81). They asked Wizard Ally to make up some new spells for them that would be sure to win the little gold cup.

So Ally said out loud, 'Scotland will win the World Cup.' He said this so many times that the land became enchanted! He had a jester, called Rod Stewart, who sometimes visited his castle. He made loud noises that people called songs. He sang Ally's new spell to everybody, and it went like this: 'Ole, Ola, Ole, Ola. We're going to bring that gold cup from over there.' The words weren't very catchy, but the magic was so powerful that everybody who lived north of a big river called the Tweed got tremendously excited. They all wanted to go to Argentina with Wizard Ally. They called themselves the Tartan Army. Every day the Scottish newspapers printed the sayings of Wizard Ally, and the Tartan Army became dizzy with excitement.

Before he flew off to the fairyland, Wizard Ally just had time to think of the names of some players. He called them his team. But, sad to say, when he got to Argentina none of his magic spells seemed to work. There was such a noise coming from the spells of all the other football wizards there that everything got muddled up in his head, and he forgot which players could do what.

For example, he completely forgot he had a very clever player called Graham Souness in his squad, and didn't even let him sit on something called 'the bench'. He also forgot to go and watch the first team Scotland had to play against, Peru, to see if they had any special magic. Ally was very surprised to find they had two very fast and brilliant wingers, called Munante and Oblitas, who ran round and round his full backs and made them giddy. But he did have one very cunning trick: at half-time, he told his goalkeeper, Alan Rough, to kick the ball further downfield. A naughty pixie had stolen Rough's magic boots, though, so Scotland lost. Next, their speedy, jinking, elusive winger, Jimmy Johnstone was found with some magic potion he wasn't supposed to have, and he was thrown out of the fairyland.

Could things get worse? They could. Scotland played Iran next. Everybody knew they were useless and were only in the fairyland by mistake, but Ally's spells refused to work. The more he said, 'We're going to win the Cup' the crosser the Tartan Army became, and when Scotland could only draw 1–1 with Iran some of them wanted their money back! In Scotland, to say such a thing nearly always stops all magic spells from working.

But then a bunch of sorcerers in grey suits began consulting mysterious symbols and figures. They said that, if Scotland beat Holland by three clear goals, they could stay in this fairyland. Otherwise they must be as silent as

Trappist monks for at least the next four years. Wizard Ally threw away his spell book. He picked Souness, told Kenny Dalglish he was the best striker in the world and Scotland went out and played like angels. In the first half, they conceded a penalty but, just before half-time, Souness crossed to Joe Jordan, who headed down for Dalglish to volley a thrilling goal. Scotland now had to win 4–1. Within a minute of the restart, Scotland won a penalty. Two–one. Could they do it, even at this late hour?

For a while we thought they could. Archie Gemmill produced some magic of his own to beat three men and make it 3–1. Not only the Tartan Army were rubbing their eyes. Even in the press boxes the reporters were on their feet cheering. Just one more goal! And then, and then . . .

From almost thirty metres, Holland's Johnny Rep hit the shot of a lifetime. Alan Rough launched himself like Superman in full flight, but not even he could get his fingertips to it. Three–two to Scotland, but they might just as well have lost 10–0 for all the difference it made. The performance against the Dutch had restored some pride, but Ally returned home a wiser and very much sadder man. He stopped being a wizard, burned his book of spells, and settled for a quiet life managing Motherwell, Airdrie, Ayr United and even, in a particularly humble moment, Queen of the South.

But Scotland forgave him. When he died, aged 72, he was widely mourned. 'A national treasure', he was dubbed. After all, for a few precious months he really had made his countrymen believe they could touch the stars.

Over the Parrot and Sick As a Moon

The change in interviewing techniques, 1978 onwards

In the really good old days, all of 25 years ago and not that long after George Eastham and co. had succeeded in upping a soccer player's wage from about five bob a week, live interviews were conducted with proper decorum.

Scene 1: October 1978. Intrepid BBC reporter untangles himself from sundry trailing wires on the edge of Goodison Park, and steps forward for an in-depth probe into the thoughts of the hero of the moment, Everton striker Andy King. King had just scored the only goal in the local Merseyside derby with Liverpool and would, the reporter assumed, be keen to explain to a waiting nation exactly how he'd managed it. Liverpool were, after all, rather good at the time.

REPORTER (showing an early ability for stating the blindingly obvious): Andy King.

ANDY KING: Would you get off the pitch please?

REPORTER (probably tugging forelock, though this is not on record): Congratulations.

ANDY KING: Thanks.

Compelling stuff, showing the composure and awareness of a supreme athlete moments after his triumph; and a properly deferential attitude in the would-be interviewer, even if his bosses had hoped for something more – what shall we say? – searching. Now fast-forward quarter of a century to see how things have improved.

Scene 2: Intrepid BBC reporter interviews Dundee United chief executive, Jim McLean. Behind him are the usual bits of white plywood liberally pasted with the ubiquitous logos seen weekly, and instantly forgotten, as various players and/or managers either struggle for a cliché or look around with swivelling eyes for a way out.

REPORTER: How long do you give Alex Smith to get it right on the park?

McLEAN (with a more than reasonable enquiry of his own): You think I'm going to answer a stupid question like that?

REPORTER (showing that in 25 years the skill of stating the obvious is alive and well): I'm only asking it.

McLEAN: I told you before I wouldn't be ******* answering it. And make sure that's cut . . . I'll tell you something else. (Sound of bone forcefully striking flesh.) Don't ever ******* offer me that again.

There's a pleasing directness about this interview that must have had the producer purring. OK, there was a decision about whether or not to put it out before the watershed, and the Corporation may have had to pay for private healthcare overnight. But, as a piece of investigative reporting into the strategy and tactics making Dundee United what they were at the time, what more could you want?

I do have a question of my own, though, and maybe you share it. It's at its worst in soccer, but why is it that nearly all sports interviewing seems to lie midway between the inane and the half-witted? There are plenty of articulate players, coaches and managers around and by and large the general population is decently educated. How many more generations have to pass before post-match interviews are conducted on the level of consenting adults rather than mentally challenged kids?

'An Ageing Hero and an Embarrassed Transgressor'

Manchester City v Tottenham Hotspur, the 100th FA Cup final, 1981

If you want to be remembered, what better moment to choose than the 100th FA Cup final? When he woke up that morning, Manchester City's 33-year-old Tommy Hutchinson couldn't have foreseen his sad destiny. Had he stopped to reflect on Spurs' strange affinity with the FA Cup in years ending with a 1 (see page 16), he might have gone out and bought a lucky horseshoe.

This was the immensely creative Spurs team of Ossie Ardiles, Ricky Villa and Glen Hoddle in midfield with Garth Crooks and Steve Archibald up front, a team 'earnestly attempting to produce sophisticated football', as Geoffrey Green summed them up. Manchester City knew their only real hope, short of a lightning strike, lay in taking possession of the midfield, by force if necessary, and controlling it. They succeeded better than they could have dared to hope and, at the end of thirty torrid minutes for the Spurs defence, Hutchinson scored with – unusually for him – a well-directed header. Try as they might, Spurs could not wrest control away from City, and Ricky Villa, so often their inspiration and talisman, was unable to find the key to win more of the ball.

With 22 minutes remaining, Villa was substituted and the change seemed to bring Spurs to life. At last they began to sweep forward, pressing the City goal and bringing a sequence of superb saves from Joe Corrigan. With ten minutes remaining, and Corrigan seemingly on the path to canonisation, Spurs won a free kick on the edge of the area when Ardiles was pulled down by Gow. Ardiles tapped the ball to Hoddle, who aimed to curl it round the right-hand end of the defensive wall. As the ball left his foot, Hutchinson broke early from the wall, and the kick, which seemed to be going wide, glanced off his right shoulder past the wrong-footed Corrigan and into the far corner of the net. The score stayed at 1–1 and poor Tommy Hutchinson, who had been 'an ageing hero' an hour earlier, was now 'an embarrassed transgressor', the only name on the score sheet. Not since the Charlton–Derby final of 1946 had a player scored at both ends.

Five days later, they were all back at Wembley for an outstanding replay. Ricky Villa, who had been angry and upset when he was substituted, scored twice while Tommy, try as he might, could not get the ball in the net at either end, let alone both. Spurs won the replay 3–2, and Hutchinson probably resolved never to join another defensive wall as long as he played.

Cobblers!

France v West Germany,
World Cup semi-final, 1982

If ever a fairytale was stood on its head, this was it. This semi-final was between Beauty (France) and the Beast (West Germany), but, instead of turning into a handsome prince, the ugly Beast grew more hideous as the game progressed. France had been playing their football with such dash and flair that all impartial onlookers wanted to see them win the Jules Rimet Trophy. By contrast, West Germany had played sterile, cynical football to grind their way into the semi-final. By the time they got there they had no friends other than those within their own borders. When the match ended, even some of their diehards were silenced by shame.

The match turned on one appalling incident in the second half, perpetrated by the German goalkeeper, Harald Schumacher – a name that translates into English, rather fittingly, as cobbler. France had just sent on substitute Patrick Battiston when Michel Platini played a beautifully angled pass into his path. As the German defence was caught flat-footed, Battiston broke clean through and a decisive score seemed inevitable as he slipped the ball round Schumacher and sidestepped him ready to turn the ball into the net. Schumacher launched himself at Battiston and felled him with a vicious forearm smash.

He was unconscious for three minutes before they got him onto a stretcher and away to hospital for treatment to his jaw, broken in two places, and his mouth, now minus two teeth. Courtesy of TV replays, many millions around the world had instant access to one of the worst assaults in soccer's history. Dropping a clanger that belied belief, the referee, however, claimed to have seen nothing and heard nothing. Not so much as a limp admonitory finger was waggled at the Butcher of Seville, as Schumacher was thereafter christened. The obliging referee simply awarded a goal kick. Had Schumacher's attack taken place outside the stadium, he would very properly have been convicted of assault and GBH, and gone down for several years. Instead the match went to extra time and Germany shaded it.

They were probably the most disdained finalists in World Cup history, and no one regretted their fall at the last hurdle. They say the sins of the father are visited on the next generation. Twenty years later a very different kind of German goalkeeper faced Brazil in the World Cup final. Oliver Kahn was brilliant, and highly respected as man, player and captain. Germany's appearance in the final owed much to his outstanding performances en route. But in the 2002 final it was his fatal blunder that gifted a goal to Brazil and gave them the confidence to go on and win. Fate had chosen the wrong German as its plaything.

'The Heaviest of Underdogs'

Liverpool v Wimbledon, FA Cup final, 1988

Wimbledon, of course, does not exist. Officially it's just part of the Borough of Merton and that, in turn, is somewhere or other in the sprawl of London south of the Thames. Back in 1955 Wimbledon, the soccer team that is, were in the Isthmian League and if you wonder what that was (other than the kind of sneeze you wouldn't want all over you on the top deck of a bus) you'd be in very good company. That was in the past.

In the 1980s (to the surprise of many, it must be admitted) they were up in the top flight famous – or infamous – for their long ball game, which at least had the virtue of being simple. Nevertheless, nobody gave them a hope in the Cup final against mighty Liverpool, then at their Rolls-Roycean best, although quite a few were pleased to see them at Wembley. There, they felt sure, they would get their comeuppance, and their unattractive approach to the game would be exposed. The bookies' odds were 4–1 on Liverpool, the clearest favourites since World War II. As Stuart Jones said in *The Times*, Wimbledon were 'the heaviest of underdogs'. He didn't, alas, explain how you weighed an underdog. Had he done so, soccer fans everywhere could have had hours of innocent amusement wrangling over the tonnage of their local dog of a team.

Wimbledon's only realistic hope was to throw such a blanket over Liverpool, and over John Barnes in particular, that they were denied any space to work in. The manager Bobby Gould and the coach Don Howe evolved a brilliant tactical plan to achieve this, and the Wimbledon players stuck to it well. As the post-match reports said, with echoes of the 1960s and the condemnation of the Italian *catenaccio* system, 'Instead of constructing their own ideas, Wimbledon destroyed Liverpool's.' Beautiful it certainly was not, but effective beyond question as Liverpool were slowly and surely dragged down to Wimbledon's level.

The game turned on clangers nevertheless, in particular a couple in quick succession in the 35th and 36th minutes. The Dons' midfielder, Thorn, 'nudged' Beardsley in the area, but he recovered well enough to put the ball in the net. The only snag was that referee Hill had already blown for a free kick to Liverpool. Now being on the receiving end of a Wimbledon 'nudge' in the 1980s – remember, this was Vinnie Jones's outfit – could give you the impression you'd collided with a tank on battle manoeuvres and, since referees were aware of Wimbledon's straightforward approach to ball possession, they tended to have their whistles at the ready.

Mr Hill was big enough to admit afterwards he'd made a mistake, but that was too late to console Liverpool. Barely sixty seconds later, a linesman waved an admonitory flag for a Liverpool challenge on Phelan that he thought (later evidence suggested he was wrong) was unfair. Dennis Wise – yes, that one – took the free kick and Sanchez rose above the throng to loop a glancing header over Grobbelaar for the only goal of the match. Liverpool still had plenty of time, though, and it took a couple of exceptional saves from Ray Houghton and Alan Hansen by the Dons' tall goalkeeper, Dave Beasant, to keep them ahead until the final clanger was dropped.

Mr Hill gave Liverpool a penalty for what he deemed a foul by Clive Goodyear on John Aldridge. It was a harsh decision, possibly owing something to the referee's awareness that he'd cancelled a perfectly good goal in the first half. Aldridge was Liverpool's penalty taker, and he'd never yet missed one for them. 'Aldridge usually does a little shuffle to see if the goalkeeper moves,' said Dave Beasant later. 'He didn't do it so much this time, so I thought he was going to put it to my left, so that's where I went.'

He certainly did, at full stretch, and straight into the history books as the first to save an FA Cup final penalty. Conversely, Aldridge became the first to miss one. Nor had Dave Beasant finished with the record books. As he climbed the steps to the royal box he became the first keeper to raise the Cup as the winning captain.

Billy the Fish Faces the Decision of His Life

Barnton v Fulchester United, Cup final, 1989

With only seconds left on the clock, the *Viz* fans crammed into Wembley held their breath as the Barnton No. 9 stepped forward to take the last-minute penalty. Their heroes, Fulchester United, led 1–0. All that stood between them and an agonising period of extra time was Billy Thomson, the wonder goalkeeper, half boy, half fish. And a forty-pound bomb strapped to the ball. Barnton's beefy No. 9 struck the ball perfectly, and as it streaked towards the top right-hand corner of the goal the crowd gasped.

Billy had a desperate choice. Either he could save the penalty and the Cup, or he could save himself. All round a hushed Wembley, people turned to their neighbours muttering, 'It's a tough decision for the young lad.' Not for a second did Billy hesitate. Throwing his fishlike body towards the top left-hand corner of his net, he finned the ball round the post and, with a deafening explosion, the Cup was heading to Fulchester!

Or was it? As Billy lay dying in his hospital bed, officials arrived to point out that bombs were not allowed on the field of play. The penalty was therefore illegal and must be retaken to determine whether the Cup was Fulchester's, or whether Barnton could earn the right to extra time. Once more, the crowd flocked in its millions to the historic stadium, hastily repaired for the occasion. The minute boy/fish keeper lay on the line, attached to his life-support system. This time it was Barnton's massive No. 7 who stepped up to hit the ball like a pile driver. For what seemed like minutes, time stood still as the crowd held its breath – they were good at that in those days – and people turned to their neighbours asking 'Can the boy/fish wonder rise from his deathbed to save it?' Desperately, Billy struggled for one last spasm of strength and then, with a mighty effort and a groan that echoed round the hushed stadium, hurled himself upwards to head the ball clear.

Viz fans everywhere went mad with joy as the Fulchester players hugged each other triumphantly. But where was Billy? they suddenly asked themselves. There, on his line, lay the inert body of the scaly hero. But as the Boss, balding Tommy Brown, said as he scooped up the lifeless corpse 'Wherever men gather to talk of football or fish, they will toast the name of Billy Johnson, er, Thomson.'

El Condor is Winged

Brazil v Chile, 1990 World Cup qualifier, 2nd Leg

Bill Shankly's famous dictum that soccer is more important than life or death may be taken as a merry quip in Britain (though with Shankly you could never be sure) but in Latin America they know exactly what he meant. After all, Honduras and El Salvador went to war over a soccer match, and in 1978 the Argentine government knew its fate was sealed if the country didn't reach the final in its own backyard and acted, or so it was believed, accordingly. Brazil and Chile had quite a bit of previous when they learned they were to meet in a home-and-away qualifying tie for the 1990 World Cup finals, so things were not entirely overflowing with milk and honey when they finally took to the pitch.

The first leg, in Santiago, Chile, had ended as a bad-tempered draw. The return, in Rio's famous Marcana stadium, required Brazil to draw or Chile to win for one or the other to go through. To universal astonishment, the game was relatively even-tempered and yellow cards remarkably few until, in the second half, Brazil went 1–0 up. If you have had the experience of being at a game in the Marcana, you will remember (fondly if you were a neutral observer, or with alarm if you were following the losing team) the deafening drum-beating, flag-waving, cracker-exploding, party-erupting scenes that can follow a popular goal. They did now. Amid the din and exultation, a firework flew out of the crowd onto the pitch with a satisfying amount of smoke and flame. And, lo!, as the smoke cleared, there lay the inert form of El Condor, the Chilean goalkeeper, otherwise known as Roberto Rojas, with a theatrical amount of blood flowing from

99

a head wound. The Chilean team responded with predictable histrionics and left the field, never to return.

Over in Santiago, Chileans stormed the Brazilian embassy and laid waste anything in their path and, more to the point, began demanding a replay on a neutral ground. Over to poor old FIFA to wrestle with the problem of which government might fall following its team's failure to qualify.

But wait a minute. Something wasn't quite right. Keen observers, especially if they were Brazilian, pointed out that the firework had landed quite some distance from El Condor. Not quite a pitch length, to be sure, but the distance of a short lay-off. And just what kind of deadly firework was it that had such powerful explosive effect? Examination of its remains showed it to be a fairly harmless flare. So how could it have produced so much blood? El Condor's head came in for scrutiny. Not a burn or a scorch mark could be found, only evidence that it had been tampered with by person or persons unknown employing 'a sharp instrument'. That was enough for FIFA. Out went Chile for their refusal to complete the match, and Brazil were on their way to Italy.

El Condor was instructed to appear before FIFA to explain himself, and was brought to ground in a flurry of feathers and pinions. The result was a lifetime ban from ever having a spherical object in his nest again. In time he opened his beak and told the truth of what happened. He admitted that he'd tucked a scalpel into his glove in case things went badly and the opportunity for a melodramatic spot of self-mutilation presented itself. They did and it did, but it all went much, much further than he'd intended. He loved his football, was distraught at his banishment, and turned to religion.

Austria Gets a Faer-Oeld Thumping

Faeroe Islands v Austria, Landskrona, Sweden, 1990

By no means the worst team in the world, Austria, although their performance in the 1990 World Cup had been rather below expectation. It looked, however, as though fate had been kind to them in their qualifying group for the 1992 European Championship. There it was in black and white: an away tie against the Faeroe Islands, pop. 45,000.

True, getting there might be a problem, since no one seemed to know quite where the Faeroe Islands were. Up north somewhere, left a bit, back a bit, up a bit more – somewhere about there was the general opinion. The Faeroes solved the problem by arranging for 'home' to be transferred, for the purposes of the game, to Sweden. As this was to be their very first competitive soccer match, it seemed only kind to conceal from their opponents that they didn't actually have any grass pitches to play on in their true home.

They didn't seem to have much by way of any players either. Their captain, Joannes Jakobsen, was a dentist's manager who did a spot of folk singing when the mood was on him. They could also boast a car salesman, who had time to practise, since he rarely worked overtime on a small island with a limited population and a shortage of roads. Then there was the local fishmonger, who made a good living as he purveyed the staple diet, a bank clerk, a baker, a carpenter and a

101

goalkeeper called Jens Knudsen, who sported a fetching line in hand-knitted woolly hats.

All in all, much though they enjoyed their soccer, their short-term objective was to avoid humiliation and their longer goal to get up to the standards of, say, Finland a few years down the road. Those European sports journalists who had noticed the tie was to take place didn't wish to hurt the feelings of the Faeroese, so recently admitted to membership of FIFA, and limited their warnings of apocalypse to something around the 5–0 mark, while privately fearing much worse. A local hack, ever the optimist, said that if the Faeroes avoided defeat, he would happily walk all the way home.

Come the big day the Austrians trotted out, determined not to look cocky. Just as well, because by half-time they had failed to penetrate the defence of the miscellaneous students, bakers, fishmongers etc., let alone the woolly hat of Jens Knudsen as he flung himself around between the posts, and there was no score.

Eighteen minutes into the second half, the dam burst, but not at the expected end. Torkil Nielsen strolled through the middle of the admittedly mediocre Austrian defence and planted the ball politely but firmly in the back of their net. And 1–0 the score remained to the end. The local journalist who hadn't dared predict anything so far-fetched as a draw duly walked all the way home without bothering to adopt sackcloth and ashes. He took off all his gear and made the trip in his birthday suit. Just to prove their opening shot was no fluke, the Faeroes then rolled up to Belfast for their next game and drew 1–1 with Northern Ireland.

Is this a good moment to ask why we, in the so-called 'big' soccer nations, lay out such vast sums of money for players who seem incapable of doing any better than the part-timers of the Faroes?

Gazza Needs a Second Box of Kleenex

Nottingham Forest v Tottenham Hotspur, FA Cup final, 1991

The first time Paul Gascoigne gained widespread public attention was when he was groped by Vinnie Jones in a League game between Wimbledon and Newcastle. An alert photographer captured the moment Vinnie's wandering hands fastened on to something warm and tender and Gazza sprang – in more senses than one – into general recognition. The tears in his eyes on that occasion became something of a career theme.

He had hardly wiped them away after his lachrymose exit from Italia 1990 when he had a something else to blub about. Gazza's World Cup tears could at least be blamed on German provocation above and beyond what an impressionable Geordie lad could reasonably be expected to bear. The second occasion was entirely his own fault. By now with Spurs, he had played brilliantly en route to Wembley, especially in the semi-final defeat of their north London rivals, Arsenal, and his reward was a first Cup final appearance, against Notts Forest.

As it transpired, Gazza's clanger was by no means the only one to be dropped in this final, but it was certainly the most spectacular. The game was less than quarter of an hour old when he launched himself feet first in an airborne attack – sage opinion thought he was attempting a tackle – on Forest defender Gary Charles. In a nightclub brawl it would have been an horrendous challenge. In an organised sporting contest it was unforgivable. According to Gary Lineker, also in the Spurs' side, Gazza 'was hyped up before the game and needed a way to release all that energy'. This is an interesting defence, and it would be instructive to hear the Lord Chief Justice's view when trying someone at the Old Bailey for GBH. 'I know I nearly killed him, your honour, but I was just releasing some energy. Please can I go now?' 'Yes, in five years' time' would probably be the response.

Fortunately for Gary Charles, Gazza's energy levels were so high he managed a passable impression of a cartoon character as he sailed through his intended victim and crash-landed in Wembley's famously clinging turf. The ref had no need to grope in his pocket for a red card. Gazza was transported off on a stretcher with torn cruciate ligaments and paid a heavy price for his recklessness. He was out of the game for months, his intended transfer to Lazio was put on hold and, as Lineker said, 'he was never really the same player again after that'. Stuart Pearce lined up the resulting free kick. He hit it like a whiplash beyond the Spurs keeper, Thorsvedt, and into the net 'before the six-strong wall had wheeled around to discover its fate' (said the Nottingham Forest website).

The ref dropped the next clanger, disallowing a Gary Lineker goal for offside when everyone, including Brian Clough and the Forest supporters, agreed it was legitimate. Minutes later, Lineker fluffed a penalty but Spurs eventually managed a deserved equaliser in the 55th minute, when Paul Stewart found space on the right and scored with an angled shot.

The stage was set for the final drama in extra time. Des Walker had been having a brilliant game in Forest's defence, denying Lineker space and marking him virtually out of the match, but, at the end, it all went horribly and undeservedly wrong for him. He had never scored a goal, not for England, nor in the league and certainly not in the Cup. Now he rose, literally, to the occasion on the grandest of all stages, a Wembley final. Under pressure from, ironically, Gary Mabbutt (whose own goal in 1987 saw the Cup go to Coventry) he leaped to head over the bar. That, at least, was the intention as he left Mother Earth. Unfortunately he jumped a split second too early, and instead of a heroic save he managed a well-directed flick just under the bar. Keeper Mark Crossley had had an afternoon to remember, including a penalty save, but this was one angle from which he had not been expecting to come under attack and the Cup was on its way back to White Hart Lane.

Gary Stubs His Toe

England v Brazil, Wembley, 1992

Just one more goal. That's all Gary Lineker needed to catch Bobby Charlton's record of 49 goals for England as he approached the end of his illustrious career. He had scored against France, the CIS and, memorably, Poland to see England into the final stages of the 1992 European Cup. Now, in a preparatory friendly against Brazil at Wembley, he stepped up to the penalty spot after being fouled – or so referee Jim McCluskey reckoned, though TV replays left room for doubt – by goalkeeper Carlos Gallo.

Gary had landed four penalties for England, but in recent times his touch from the spot had been wavering a little. In the 1991 Cup final he had fluffed a Spurs penalty chance against Notts Forest, and in the semi-finals of the 1991–2 League Cup he had again had a chance to beat Forest's Mark Crossley. He'd succeeded, but only with a very high-risk strategy. Instead of picking top left or right, or bottom left or right, and belting the stuffing out of the ball, he had run up, let Crossley dive like a hopeful dolphin in the direction he'd probably decided on in advance, and then chipped it with extreme delicacy into the middle of the net.

Confronted by Carlos Gallo, he reached into his memory bank and remembered what a pleasure it had been to float the ball over the very spot the goalkeeper had been keeping warm only seconds earlier. He thought he rather liked the sensation, and reckoned that word of his devious approach was unlikely to have been widely advertised in Brazil. He trotted up and Carlos obligingly fell to his right and assumed a recumbent position.

Unfortunately, Gary stubbed his toe in the turf. The ball flopped feebly forward, and Carlos leaped enthusiastically to his feet and pounced on it.

Gary Lineker played in another six matches for England but didn't score again, and Bobby Charlton's record remained inviolate. Ironically, Charlton had hoped to retire with a round fifty for England, and you could say it was a penalty miss against Scotland in 1960 that prevented him from reaching the target. After that miss, he was stood down as England's penalty taker. Another fifteen penalties were awarded to Charlton's England side, but he was never again invited to convert one.

Pompey Pay the Penalty

Liverpool v Portsmouth, FA Cup semi-final, 1992

Back in 1992 patience finally ran out on endless replays of drawn Cup games. Never mind that some of the most thrilling encounters had gone to three or even four replays as two evenly matched teams probed each other's weaknesses over, say, 360 minutes of playing time and brought the crowds packing in. The new paymasters, the television companies, couldn't be expected to go on changing their schedules simply because people enjoyed the tension and the cut and thrust of footballing skills, could they, now? Dear me, no. Instant gratification and on to the next round, that's the thing my boy. Learn to live with the times.

So sudden death by penalty shootout was decreed. A few seconds of vicarious pleasure and a few drops of blood on the grass that could soon be mopped up was deemed preferable to taking the trouble to find out which was the better side.

The first game in England to which the new ruling was applied was a semi-final replay between Portsmouth and Liverpool at Villa Park. Pompey's manager at the time was Jim Smith, and he drew up a list of penalty takers just in case the worst should come to the worst (it did: Liverpool equalised with three minutes to go). Unfortunately, a spate of last-minute withdrawals made nonsense of the list, and hapless stand-ins had to be hurriedly organised. It didn't make much difference. Pompey hadn't spent any time practising penalties, with or without their original choices.

Alan Knight was Portsmouth's keeper that day. He hadn't practised saving any penalties either, and he duly let in four. Having never seen a video of the shootout – too painful – he cheerfully admits he probably dived the wrong way for every one of them. He didn't, in fact. For Ian Rush's he dived hopefully in the right direction, but was beaten anyway. Should sides put in plenty of practice taking penalties? 'It's handy if you know who your penalty takers are going to be,' says Knight, 'but ultimately it's just a matter of whether a player chokes or not. All I know is that some poor bugger will miss one!' That's certainly one way of looking at it, and a very relaxed one, too. In 1992, Pompey were so relaxed they lost the penalty lottery 4–1, and Liverpool went on to beat Sunderland in the final.

Twelve years on, Portsmouth were up against Liverpool in the fifth round. A draw meant a replay was needed, and the denizens of Fratton Park could not suppress a sinking sensation, in the pits of their stomachs, that history might repeat itself. Not so the team. With two days to go, they still hadn't bothered with any penalty-taking practice and Shaka Hislop hadn't got his knees dirty rehearsing any saves from the spot. Half-time came with the score 0–0, and Portsmouth nerves were that little bit tighter. But they needn't have worried. This time they won 1–0 and, in an ironic twist of fate, Liverpool's Michael Owen missed a penalty in the 63rd minute that might, if he'd scored, have taken the game to extra time – and even, perhaps, another penalty shootout!

'I Play in a Mad Position'

Everton v Liverpool, 1993

Funny chap, Bruce Grobbelaar. Didn't always seem to remember which side he was playing on. Like the little girl with the curl, when he was good, he was very, very good, but when he was bad he was horrid. One of his horrid moments occurred in the 1993 Merseyside derby at Goodison Park. On the receiving end was not a villainous Everton forward doing his best to violate Bruce's virgin net (though it was ravished, twice) but one of his own mates in red, the young and partially innocent Steve McManaman.

Week in, week out, from the terraces and on TV replays, you see goalkeepers shouting and gesticulating furiously at their own side. Any incursion of the other side into their own half, never mind their own penalty area, is treated as an offence on a par with homicide, and directed personally at them. Like medieval religious fanatics wandering the land whipping themselves, many seem to think they carry the sins of all mankind on their shoulder, and they complain about it unceasingly.

Bruce was up there among the best of them on many occasions, but Goodison 1993 set a new benchmark. Just short of the half-hour, Everton had a corner, a weak affair that McManaman failed to clear properly. Everton's Mark Ward seized on the ball and slapped it past Grobbelaar, whereupon young Steve found his own keeper chasing him down the pitch like a heffalump after a pot of Pooh's honey. Cornering him, Bruce let fly with mouth and hands, doing a passable imitation of Tigger on unmentionable substances. He landed a slap, and was lining up a punch when Steve wisely ducked, and then slapped him back. Everton players hugged themselves happily, enjoying the spectacle no end but uncertain whether the rules allowed the laying of mid-match bets.

'We weren't just beaten, we were terrible. Second best in everything,' snarled Bruce as he left Goodison after the match, steam still billowing from his ears. The Sunday tabloids enjoyed a predictable field day at 'Bruiser Bruce's' expense, but the Liverpool manager Graham Souness sounded as if he sympathised. 'I want players who show passion,' he said. But when, after a few days, he calmed down Grobbelaar explained how the whole unfortunate misunderstanding had occurred: 'I was mad, but I play in a mad position,' he confided. That's all right, then. But it's a warning to young players: be careful whom you share the bath with after a game. Do a quick sanity test before you're drowned for a back pass that wasn't inch-perfect.

An Unqualified Catastrophe

World Cup qualification goes awry, 1993

The autumn of 1993 proved to be a bad month for those hoping to join the final stages of the 1994 World Cup. Japan needed to beat Iraq in their final qualifying game and on the outcome rested not only their hopes of a place in the last 32, but of being the sole host of the Cup scheduled for 2002. Their Iraqi opponents enjoyed a high domestic profile, being managed by none other than Uday Hussein, son of Saddam, who despite his lack of experience in the Premiership, had a novel range of incentive schemes including electric shocks, cattle prods and the occasional well-directed bullet. Consequently Iraq had already been eliminated collectively from the competition, and would be taken care of individually at a later date.

Leading 2–1 with a matter of seconds remaining, Japan nevertheless contrived to concede a last-gasp goal. In the ensuing silence back home you could have heard a rice paper drop as it sank into the national consciousness that this meant co-hosting the 2002 World Cup with South Korea, a neighbour well down the pecking order of those the Japanese would willingly clasp to their bosoms.

France, meanwhile, were being hailed as one of the strongest and most attractive teams around, and likely to be eventual winners of the Cup itself. Qualifying should be no more than a practice workout. All they needed was a quick win over the unfancied Israelis or a draw against Bulgaria, both games at home in Paris. Unfortunately they dropped a clanger – with some force – on their own toes when, having led the Israelis 2–1 at half-time and, indeed, with only five minutes of full time remaining, they lost 2–3. Ah, well, said the French with a Gallic shrug, or something similar. Bring on Bulgaria. So they did.

All went well at first. France took a 1–0 lead, but lost it to see the score tied at 1–1. Still, a draw was good enough as they ran down the clock and when, in the dying seconds, they won a free kick in Bulgaria's half they seemed to have qualification as tightly buttoned up as public information about President Mitterand's mistress. Unfortunately they failed to take account of David Ginola's talent for the unexpected. That, at least, is a polite Anglo-Saxon way of putting it. Ginola decided this was the moment to showcase his glittering ball skills. Instead of taking thirty seconds to debate the precise spot from which to take the kick, followed by an attempt to land the ball in the Champs Elysées, he took a quick one and shimmied off down the wing. He was promptly dispossessed by the solid Bulgars, who broke upfield and scored, whereupon the referee blew for the end of the game and, for that matter, of France's qualification.

Ginola was greeted by his compatriots with the forthright language normally reserved for lunatics and foreigners and was forced to take refuge in England, where he developed a lucrative career advertising hair tonic on television with occasional bursts of soccer in between.

When the Red in Black Saw Red

Crystal Palace v Manchester United, 1995

Ooh, la la, Cantona! Eric the Red was playing in all black on the fateful day Manchester United travelled down to London for what should have been a routine execution of Crystal Palace. It was a time when United kept the tills ringing by changing their away strip more quickly than British Rail put up the price of tickets in order to goad parents into buying new shirts for the kids as often as possible – Christmas, Easter, Valentine's Day, Mother's Day, you name it, what about some new away shirts?

On this particular day, United were black all over, with lovely shiny gold numbers on their backs. When they could take their minds off next week's fetching colour scheme, they were also well in line for their third consecutive championship title and another Cup final at Wembley.

Meanwhile, in the front row of the stalls, as it were, was one of those spectators who delight in taunting players with more talent in their big toes than they have in their whole bodies. He had a name, but, as he got more publicity at the time than he should have had, why give him any more now? Eric the Red (except he was in black at the time) was used to this kind of behaviour, but there comes a time when enough is enough, especially when you've just been sent off (again) and are on your way to test the temperature of the water. As a volley of insults flew towards him, Cantona felt that time had arrived. He was a superb striker who missed little, even without the ball, as he demonstrated with a graceful, kung-fu, feet-first vault across the low rail into the offending loudmouth's midriff.

The tabloids kept themselves predictably amused for days with the tale (the *Sun* smeared it across eleven pages in order to protect us from anything as exhausting as thought) and went into their usual lather of self-righteousness. Officialdom then chugged into ponderous action. First, Cantona's club had a go, then the FA and finally the courts. Fines, strictures, suspensions (from playing rather than by the thumbs), condemnations and lectures followed hard on each other's heels for an offence that, had it been committed in a pub, would have resulted in a quick flurry, a sharp 'ouch' and the end of the matter. Meanwhile, back at Old Trafford, the will to live hadn't exactly been extinguished, but United's capabilities had been severely wounded. They lost out to Blackburn in the title race and to Everton in the Cup final, and there was general agreement that it was the loss of Cantona's services that had cost them so dear.

There was widespread expectation that Eric the Red would turn his back on England and United and, like one of his own eccentric quotations, imitate a seagull and follow the trawler back to France. In fact, with plenty of idle time for reflection, he did not. The following season, with Cantona to the fore, United claimed back the Championship. Meanwhile, the 'fan' in the front row was himself charged with incitement, fined and banned from soccer grounds, whereupon, in imitation of his original victim, he attempted to duff up the solicitor on the prosecution's side and found himself admiring the decor of a prison cell.

What Goes Up Must Come Down – Somewhere

Arsenal v Real Zaragoza, European Cup Winners' Cup, 1995; Brazil v England, World Cup quarter-final, 2002

I wonder what David Seaman was thinking about as the very last European Cup Winners' Cup wound towards its uneventful, scoreless conclusion, and he strolled around his area with half an eye on the play weaving its deadlocked way from one side of centre field and back to the other. The England fast bowler, 'Typhoon' Tyson, who destroyed Australia down under half a century ago, would recite Wordsworth to himself as he trudged back to the end of his run-up. 'I wandered lonely as a cloud – think I'll pop a short one into the ribcage next – when all at once I saw . . .' But that doesn't sound quite like Safe Hands, as David was known. More likely, he was contemplating the inevitable penalty shootout to follow, and wondering if he'd return to Highbury a hero.

In the middle distance and over on the right-hand touchline, Nayim had got his studs on the ball. Now with Real Zaragoza, he had formerly played for Spurs and as the whole of north London – i.e. the world – knows there's a striking deficiency of love and TLC between Arsenal and Spurs. It was therefore axiomatic that if he could win the Cup for Real he'd not only be flavour of the year in Zaragoza, but back at White Hart Lane as well.

So, from the halfway line he swung his right foot and dispatched the ball into orbit. Up and up it went, and levelled out to float high above the heads below. Tony Adams and his defence peered upwards as it hovered above them. Was it a bird? No, too round. Was it a zeppelin? No, too short. Finally, it began to re-enter earth's atmosphere. Safe Hands caught sight of the object as it began its descent. Nothing to waste much time on. It would clearly land in the back of the crowd. But no! With a wicked dip like a Shane Warne top-spinner, it steepened its trajectory and homed in on the goal line. Seaman began the frantic scramble to get there first. Too late. One bounce on the line and into the top of the net. 'I'm a firm believer in fate and all that stuff. Especially now,' said a chastened goalkeeper afterwards.

Fate was not by any means done with Seaman, though it wandered off to play with other people before returning seven years later, just in time for England's all-important quarter-final clash with Brazil in the 2002 World Cup. Before the knockout stages, Seaman had had a brilliant campaign, especially in the pool game with Argentina in Sapporo, where a crucial save ensured England hung on to win. Against Brazil, England played well – above expectations, indeed. They had led 1–0, and, although they conceded a goal to tie the score at 1–1, the issue was still in the balance when Brazil were awarded a free kick. As Ronaldinho lined up to take it, it seemed too far away for a direct shot on goal, and the pundits' odds were on a floated ball across the goalmouth.

What happened next – or rather *how* it happened – depends very much on whom you believe, but the end result was indisputable. From Ronaldinho's foot the ball floated across the face of the goal, as predicted, and then looped slowly – or so it seemed to the onlookers – over Safe Hands and into the top corner of the net. Two–one to Brazil, and England departed the competition, leaving their opponents to get on with winning it.

There followed much-heated debate about whether Ronaldinho had meant to score direct or whether it was all some ghastly accident. In other words, had he shot, had he slipped, or was he attempting a clever cross that had all gone wrong? As if it mattered. Naturally Ronaldinho was quite clear that he had always intended a shot of such subtlety that it would have fooled the Almighty himself – but what else would you expect him to say? It would certainly have been entertaining if he'd gone to the post-match press conference and said, 'I'm really not very good and, if the wind hadn't caught it, it would probably have hit the corner flag.' This is what he actually said, and you can believe it or not exactly as you please: 'My teammate Cafu had told me that David Seaman usually moves forward preparing to take square balls' (no, I'm not making it up). 'It was a bit far, but I tried it.'

Winners of the Cup For Cockups

Manchester City v Liverpool, Premiership, 1996

The bottom of the table had an interesting look to it as the teams
came to the very last game of the season. Here's how it appeared:

	Played	Points	Goal difference
Sheffield Wednesday	37	39	–13
Coventry City	37	37	–18
Southampton	37	37	–18
Manchester City	37	37	–25
QPR	37	33	
Bolton Wanderers	37	29	

In other words, Manchester City had to win their final game at home
against Liverpool. A draw was no use unless either Southampton or
Coventry were defeated (in the event, both fought out goalless draws).
With a sure eye for the future, Malcolm Allison, a former City manager,
had once said, 'If there were a cup for cockups, City would win it' – and it
was never more evident than in the extraordinary game that followed.

The woolly thinking that contributed to this particular cockup began
when Nigel Clough, one of the most accomplished and gutsy strikers of
the 1990s, was told to play deep in midfield. Niall Quinn, equally

determined and skilful, was graciously permitted to play as a striker but, as the disbelieving *Times* reporter at the game said the next day, 'Playing Quinn without employing wingers to give him the ball surely ranks as the most significant blunder of an error-filled season.' Quinn was taken off in the 60th minute, and in the 67th minute Clough was replaced – with a winger. One might call this shutting the door of the birdcage when the parrot's lost its beak. No wonder it felt sick later.

The first half was embarrassingly bad. Liverpool, secure in third spot whatever happened elsewhere, strolled around the field as though there were no opposition on it (indeed there wasn't very much) and, when it occurred to them, popped in a couple of goals. In the second half, things were the opposite. In a week's time Liverpool had a Cup final against Manchester United to worry about, and they appeared to stop playing altogether. City, sensing possible survival despite everything, pressed forward and scored twice to make it 2–2.

With minutes left to go, the City bench seemed satisfied that a draw was all they needed, and passed the information out to the players that they only needed to waste time and ensure it was forthcoming. Niall Quinn, listening to the radio in the dressing room, realised this was a terrible mistake and rushed down pitch-side to yell a warning. Too late. The draw was all City could manage, and down they went to the First Division. 'We've given our fans another kick in the teeth,' commented manager Alan Ball with an unusual predilection for the truth, the whole truth and nothing but the truth.

Dr Strangelove Meets David Beckham

Argentina v England, World Cup, 1998

Like endlessly bickering lovers, it seemed Argentina and England just couldn't keep away from each other. Despite the festering antagonisms, whether to do with animals (see page 63) or hands appearing in unexpected places, here they were again, on this occasion at St Etienne in France for the 1998 World Cup. This time it was a stray foot that caused the hoo-ha.

Film buffs who recall Peter Sellers's Cold War epic, *Dr Strangelove*, will remember that the ex-Nazi scientist's right arm sporadically took on a life of its own, leaping upwards into an enthusiastic 'Sieg Heil!' at moments of maximum embarrassment. In the second half of what was fast becoming an exciting contest in which England almost, but not quite, overhauled Argentina, David Beckham's right leg suffered a Strangelovean spasm. If the consequences did not involve all-out nuclear war, you could have been forgiven for failing to spot the difference when the paper dropped onto your doormat next morning.

It is a simple tale. Beckham was fouled and brought down by Diego Simeone, and the referee immediately blew for a free kick to England. Simeone was affronted in that tedious way to which we are all too well accustomed from some high-profile players, and stood arguing the toss with his back to Beckham, who was face down in St Etienne's rich and fertile soil. Despite his ideal position for a close study of grass and its growing habits, Beckham was aware that it was his tormentor whose legs he could see out of the corner of his eye, and from the raised voices must have had a pretty shrewd idea that the referee was not a million miles away either. So quite why he chose that precise moment to flick his right heel upwards and backwards must remain one of life's unsolved riddles. The outcome was, to say the least, spectacular. As Beckham's heel lightly brushed Simeone's right buttock – or was it his left? – Simeone collapsed, writhing on the turf, as though hit by a bazooka shell from the stands.

All this happened in Beckham's salad days, many hairstyles ago, before the media tumbled to the fact that he was divine – or rather that they could make more money by worshipping him than destroying him. Failing to realise he was in an august presence, the referee – who was probably fed up with so much niggling and squabbling – saw red. Or, more accurately, Beckham saw red.

Being young, a Manchester United player and, moreover, already engaged to Posh Spice, he promptly became a hate figure, and for several months was booed and roundly abused whenever he stepped onto a pitch. He bore it all with remarkable fortitude and without complaint. It is difficult to pinpoint exactly when he was transformed from sinner to saint, but the composure with which he bore his martyrdom and the undimmed levels of skill and ability he continued to parade all played their part. No more than a season passed before his clanger was forgiven and he became, for the next few years, the player everybody loved to love.

The Cup Tie That Never Took Place

Arsenal v Sheffield United, FA Cup 5th round, 1999

So you thought you were in the crowd at Highbury on Saturday, 13 February 1999 – that memorable day when Arsenal beat Sheffield United 2–1 in the fifth round of the Cup? If you think you were, you were dreaming, because the tie never took place, and that's official. Mind you, 22 players and the odd sub ran around the field for 90 minutes and goals were scored at both ends but, within half an hour of the final whistle, it was announced it all counted for nothing. It simply hadn't happened. So many wasted train fares from Sheffield; so many elaborate excuses to escape the danger of being taken shopping – all wasted.

This is what happened or, officially, didn't happen. Arsenal opened the scoring to ignite the familiar refrain of 'One–nil to the Arsenal'. Unfortunately for the neatness of the jingle, United then scored to make it 1–1. And so it remained, deadlocked, until, as Arsenal manager Arsène Wenger put it, in a line probably never before or since uttered by a manager, 'Unfortunately, we scored a second goal.' You see? You were dreaming. What on earth can have happened to create this surreal scenario?

As the game wound towards its end, United's Lee Morris went down injured. The ball found its way to the keeper Alan Kelly, who walloped it into touch to suspend play while his teammate got treatment. So far, so good. When Morris was vertical again, Arsenal's Ray Parlour took the

123

throw-in and, in a strange but nevertheless time-honoured tradition, threw the ball towards the United goal for the keeper to restart matters from the Sheffield end of the field. It was, of necessity, a long throw and, before it had got as far as Kelly's welcoming arms, Nwankwo Kanu, Arsenal's new signing from Nigeria, seized on the ball. As the bemused Kelly hesitated, he slipped it across to Marc Overmars, from Holland, who planted it emphatically in the net.

Soccer players seeking sympathetic treatment from the ref are famed for their thespian abilities, but at this point Sheffield United's players might well have been signed en masse for a Hollywood epic. As Bryon Butler wrote in the *Telegraph*, 'they thumped their chests, flailed their arms, jabbed their fingers, stamped their feet, and had a right go at the referee. Their manager Steve Bruce, the most affable of chaps, was purple with injustice.'

Was Kanu meanwhile weeping on the ground and begging forgiveness for his terrible sin? Not yet. Indeed, he had no idea what all the fuss was about. Nobody had bothered to explain to the poor chap as he stepped off the plane from Nigeria that in British soccer there is one arcane ritual, the origins long since lost in the mists of soccer's past, that has somehow survived while almost every other humane instinct has disappeared from top flight football: the idea that the opposition should be free to hoof the ball out of play, and then get it back after the trainer has been on.

Within fifteen minutes of the final whistle, Arsenal had offered to disregard the match and replay the tie at Highbury. 'I am trying to repair an accident,' said Arsène Wenger. 'Kanu is very, very sad.' Kanu tried to look very, very sad, but really seemed totally bewildered. The tie was duly replayed ten days later. The score was, once again, 2–1 to Arsenal and this time no one found cause for complaint – but a dangerous precedent had been set.

Who'll Hit the Treble Top?

Bayern Munich v Manchester United, 1999

Matt Busby was born ninety years to the day that Manchester United played Bayern Munich for the European Champions Cup at the Nou Camp in Barcelona. If this was not reason enough to regard the event as something special, they were playing a team from Munich, the city where United's greatest tragedy had befallen them in 1957. It was the city in which Duncan Edwards, Roger Byrne and many of the Busby Babes had died, but the city also where Matt himself had been drawn, gently and tenderly, out of the jaws of death and given renewed life.

There were many reasons why this was a special occasion for United, and to them could be added the fact that, if they won, they would complete an extraordinary treble: Premiership Champions, FA Cup winners and now, perhaps, European champions. But they were without Roy Keane and Paul Scholes, and they were not alone in seeking a treble. Bayern Munich were playing for stakes just as high in German terms.

The European Champions Cup stood on a dais close to the pitch, ribbons in United's colours tied to one handle, and Munich's to the other. Have a good look at the cup as you go out, Alex Ferguson had told his players, and remember how much you want it.

Only six minutes of the final had gone when Bayern Munich's Mario Basler hit a fine, low free kick through the United wall and into the net. With a 1–0 lead, the Munich defence locked into airtight place, and by half-time they were in complete command. The second half started in the same vein but, as it reached its mid-point, the pattern began to shift – not a lot, but a perceptible little. David Beckham and Nicky Butt were at last beginning to control the midfield but, up at the front, Andy Cole and Dwight Yorke still found it difficult to create clear chances. Teddy Sheringham came on as substitute with 23 minutes remaining, but with less than quarter of an hour to go it looked like curtains for United as Basler and Helmut Scholl broke clean through. Scholl lobbed Peter Schmeichel from the edge of the box – only to see the ball bounce back to Schmeichel from the inside of the post. It seemed impossible he had not scored.

Still United's pressure brought no goal. With ten minutes remaining, Ole-Gunnar Solskjaer replaced Andy Cole, yet, almost immediately, Munich broke and forced two corners. From the second, Carsten Janker hit a drive of such ferocity from only six metres that, had it been two inches lower, Schmeichel as well as the ball would have finished in the back of the net. Instead, it hit the crossbar. Somehow, for some reason, the woodwork had twice denied Munich what looked like certain goals. Was it possible that even now the footballing gods were on Manchester's side?

At the death, the physical and emotional strain was starting to show in German legs and on German faces. The inspirational but ageing Lothar Matthaus was substituted. With one minute left Basler, Mr Arrogance himself, was substituted, milking his supporters' salutes as he left, joining them in applause for the certain Munich victory. The officials guarding the Cup untied United's colours from the handle and replaced them with Munich's.

It was the ultimate provocation. If the footballing gods above did not decree punishment for such presumption, United's players did. They pressed forward one last time and won a corner. Schmeichel came sprinting upfield, with Alex Ferguson shrieking at him to get back. He ignored his manager and, for a few vital seconds, the Munich defence hesitated over how to deal with this unexpected incursion. Over came Beckham's corner. It was scrambled as far as Ryan Giggs. He tried a shot but miscued it to Sheringham, who swung round and banged it low into the net. Almost straight from the kick-off, United came streaming forward again as Munich staggered backwards. Victory had been so certain only two minutes earlier. Nowhere in their pre-match build-up had they considered the possibility of fighting to ensure extra time, if only for another ninety seconds of injury time. Solskjaer forced another corner. Beckham lined up the ball, floated it precisely onto Sheringham's head and he pushed it onto an unmarked Solskjaer. From six metres out, super-sub doesn't miss. It was 2–1.

Of all the shattered heaps of Bayern Munich humanity sprawled across the grass, Samuel Kuffour was the most despairing. He was the one who should have been marking Solskjaer. At the moment of crisis, he had made the crucial mistake. We shall never know what might have happened if the match had gone to extra time. One thing seemed certain. The gods of soccer had shown their sadistic power. They had always meant the shades of the Busby Babes to be reunited with the European Champions Cup. Along the way they had disdainfully toyed with the Mancunians – but they had reserved the real torture for poor Samuel Kuffour and his teammates.

Bring Back the Guillotine!

France makes an early exit from the World Cup, 2002

Not even on the rugby field has Gallic élan and unpredictability given its fans and admirers quite such a roller coaster ride as between 1993 and 2002. Rated the team most likely to win the 1994 World Cup, France proved more adept at finding ways of tripping over their own feet as they failed even to qualify (see page 112). In 1998, they put that nightmare behind them and showed the world just how creative and skilful they could be as they lifted the Jules Rimet Trophy in Paris. They continued on their all-conquering way as they won the European Cup in 2000, never scoring fewer than two goals per game, and thirteen all told in the tournament.

As the 2002 World Cup drew near, conclaves of pundits gravely plucked their beards and foresaw a rerun of the 1998 final between Brazil and France, in which France would become only the third nation to win the trophy in consecutive tournaments.

There were small warning signs. In 2001, France lost three friendlies in a row against Spain, Chile and Australia. Yes, that's right. Australia. The team only England lose to at soccer when normal service is running. The pundits did feel the average age of the French team was a shade on the high side, but this was flatly denied by Emanuel Petit. 'We're not too old,' he denied, flatly. The pundits realised that what they had really meant to say was that the defence was very experienced, which made all the difference. Moreover, France was spoiled for choice when it came to the attack.

There was the 'mesmerising ball wizard' (no, really, that's what they called him) Zinedine Zidane to act as playmaker, with any combination of Thierry Henry, David Trezeguet, Sylvain Wiltord and Djibril Cisse up front. 'If attack is the best means of defence, France are well placed to go all the way,' chorused the pundits. Patrick Vieira made sure everyone understood there was little point in anyone else turning up by confirming, 'We have a remarkable team with fantastic players in every position.' And to underline the meticulous thinking put into the campaign to retain the World Cup, the French coach, Roger Lemerre, revealed a secret that made even hardened journalists gasp. 'I'm not worried,' he said. 'To win a match you must score more goals than your opponents.'

Except that France didn't. To be brutally frank, they didn't score any. Not once, in any of their three Pool A matches, did the net bulge with all the promise of a French trawler landing a harvest of sardines, with or without Eric Cantona following. In the opening game of the World Cup in Seoul, Senegal turned up, as bidden, to be ritually slaughtered. They waited politely for something to happen but when, after half an hour or so, it didn't they thought they might as well start the party themselves, and Papa Bouba Diop popped one past Fabien Barthez. *Nul points* for France. 'We never thought about this scenario. What can I say?' asked the experienced 33-year-old captain, Marcel Desailly. 'We could have won but now we have to win twice.' This was a shrewd assessment that would not have struck those with less than thirty minutes' experience of watching World Cup soccer.

Indeed, things did go better in the second pool game – marginally. France did not concede a goal but nor, alas, could they quite work out how to score one. Still, a point is a point, and there was still one game to play – against Denmark – in which outright victory was essential if the champions were to move forward into the quarter-finals. This time the net bulged most fruitfully, not once but twice. Unfortunately for France, it was at the wrong end as Dennis Rommedahl in the first half, and Jon Dahl Tommason in the second, hammered the nails firmly into France's coffin. Three games played; three goals conceded; no goals scored; eleven plane tickets to Paris waiting in the changing room. As the aircraft reached cruising altitude, they could console themselves that everything Arsène Wenger had said before the opening match was true at last: 'My view is that France are above everyone else.'

Being Wise After the Event

Millwall v Sheffield United, 2003

You have to laugh. At least I think you do, though after so many repetitions the forced smile begins to hurt a bit. Dennis Wise always had a quickish sort of temper. Before the Russian Revolution, most of his career was spent with pre-czarist Chelsea and referees soon learned to keep a particular eye on Wisey. In consequence, his collection of red and yellow cards could probably paper a fair-sized room if he cared for the colour scheme. Naturally enough, the tabloid grunters soon learned to follow him out on the town to see what trouble might brew up, and were rewarded in spades when an argument with a taxi driver landed him in jail in 1995.

As age began to take its toll, Dennis moved on from Chelsea and after a turbulent year or two with Leicester found himself, aged 36, appointed as caretaker-manager of Millwall. With one toe precariously resting on the lowest rung of the managerial ladder, Dennis's first game in charge was against Sheffield United, at home in the Den. He put himself on the substitutes' bench and was very pleased with the lads as they played good football and cruised towards a 2–0 win. With five minutes of the game remaining, he felt like a bit of gentle exercise and put himself on. Three minutes later he was off again, after launching a two-footed lunge at Sheffield's Chris Armstrong. It was the thirteenth red card of his volatile career, and we won't even start on the yellows. As Mark Hodgkinson said in the *Telegraph*, 'There was a sense that what we were really watching wasn't a football match but the answer to a future pub quiz question.'

Dennis didn't argue the toss. By his own account he went up to referee Rob Styles at the end and said, 'Well done, Rob, fantastic mate.' Pretty generous stuff considering the ref had given two red cards and seven yellows in the course of the game. Humility of a kind Alex Ferguson could learn from, perhaps? And, as Dennis said to the reporters afterwards, no doubt with a grin from one ear to the other, 'I know how to entertain you lot, don't I?' There speaks a man well practised in turning a clanger to his advantage. And the best was yet to come as he took Millwall to the semi-final of the FA Cup, where they beat Sunderland and booked in for a date with Manchester United at Wembley. They lost and, but for a singularly forgiving referee, Dennis Wise would probably have earned his fourteenth red card.

'Where's the Nearest Jobcentre?'

Tottenham Hotspur v Manchester City, FA Cup 4th-round replay, 2004

As the Manchester City manager Kevin Keegan headed down the tunnel at half-time, his side trailing 3–0, he asked, 'Where's the nearest Jobcentre?' He had good reason to ask. With City languishing near the bottom of the Premiership and now being played off the park by Spurs in a fourth-round Cup replay, he ranked just about bottom in the list of Manchester's favourite citizens.

In the first half, City had been awful. Within two minutes they were a goal down, making it twelve consecutive games in which their defence had leaked a minimum of one goal. Within twenty minutes they were two down, and on the stroke of half-time they conceded a third goal as Christian Ziege scored from a free kick. As the *Daily Telegraph*'s lead football correspondent, Henry Winter, wrote the next day, 'City were so badly stalled that not even the AA would have attempted a recovery.'

Could things get any worse? You bet your life they could. When Keegan got to the dressing room he discovered he'd be playing the second half with ten men. Midfielder Joey Barton had pressed the self-destruct button. Having got a yellow card for debating the merits of Ziege's free kick with the referee, he remembered a number of other points he wished to make as the teams trudged off. So forcefully did he press his case that the ref, anxious not to let his half-time tea go cold, settled matters by giving him a second yellow and his marching orders.

Spurs began the second half convinced the game was over and gift-wrapped – with good reason after City's first-half performance. To be sure, there was a clutch of Mancunians still singing lustily 'We're going to win the Cup', but this was obviously the equivalent of a small boy whistling in the dark to keep his spirits up. Nobody still possessed of their faculties believed in a miracle – except, as it turned out, ten City players, and Shaun Wright-Phillips in particular. As he embarked on one mesmerising dribble after another through, round and across the Spurs defence, his teammates took heart. Nerves began to affect Tottenham's play, and before long they had conceded the first goal, from a free kick 25 metres out.

City kept coming forward, the numerical disadvantage evidently cancelled out since, as Keegan said later, 'Wright-Phillips did the work of two men.' Robbie Fowler, who had been tripping over his own feet before the interval, was suddenly back to the level of his glory days with Liverpool, Michael Tarnat kept playing the ball forward through gaps that no one else seemed to see, Sylvain Distin locked the defence that had been so porous in the first half, and debutant goalkeeper Arni Arason made two amazing saves in a moment of need. To say that Spurs didn't know what hit them may be an overstatement, but the assurance of the opening 45 minutes deserted them, uncertainty crept into their play and the home fans could only watch in breath-held horror as City drew level, 3–3, and extra time beckoned. Surely the unthinkable couldn't happen, could it?

It could, and it did. With the referee looking at his watch, Spurs failed to hold Tarnat down the left wing and Jon Macken met his cross perfectly to head past Kasey Keller in the Spurs goal. How high on the list of cup clangers does it rank to concede four goals to ten men? Pretty high. 'The greatest cup tie I've ever seen,' said Keegan. Well, he would, wouldn't he, but it did wonders for City. Although they failed to get past the fifth round of the Cup, they climbed away from the bottom of the table and, just six weeks later, trounced their mighty neighbours, Man

United, 4–1, in the league. It doesn't get better than that for a City fan, and all of a sudden Keegan could dare to walk the streets of Manchester again. But best not to mention the fact if you find yourself in the Tottenham half of north London.

Nervous As Kittens

Celtic v Barcelona, UEFA Cup, 4th round, 2004

Beautiful though the game can be, there are times when you shake yourself in disbelief at the antics of soccer players. Hurling yourself at the opposition is not recommended. It ends in inconvenient things such as red cards, suspension, loss of earnings, loss of the game and so on – though at least it demonstrates an ability to recognise who your opponents are. But laying into your own teammates seems a bit daft, especially if it results in your getting sent off in the middle of the match when you're not even on the field. Or maybe the problem – in these days of multi-background squads – is that the players simply don't recognise each other.

Celtic's home leg against Barcelona in the fourth round of the UEFA Cup was, the papers agreed, 'volcanic'/'wild'/'bedlam'/'tempestuous' – take your pick. Much of the trouble appeared to centre on the Barcelona midfielder Thiago Motta, who came up against a dominating performance from the Celtic defender Bobo Balde, against whom he found it nearly impossible to make the headway he assumed was his right. The fact that the twitchy German referee failed to spot a couple of nasty fouls – one of which deserved a red card – shortly before half-time may have contributed to the fire fight that erupted in the tunnel as the players left the field at the interval.

There seems to be general agreement that Motta was at the heart of the ensuing fight, and he was duly red-carded. But who or what he was attacking is still unclear – some said Celtic's Balde, others said Barca's Ronaldinho. Why he would want to set about one of his own side seems odd but there's no accounting for taste. The Celtic goalkeeper Rab

Douglas either acted as peacemaker and went to the aid of Balde and/or Ronaldinho (delete as applicable) or got stuck into Motta as well. His precise role remains shadowy, but he too found himself taking an earlier shower than planned. 'Rob is very, very annoyed,' said Celtic manager Martin O'Neill later. Well, he would be. The hot-water thermostat wasn't due to kick in for another 45 minutes.

No prizes for forecasting the look of incredulous innocence on the faces of both managers. Each was positive that his lads were whiter than the most biological of washing powders. 'It wasn't Celtic,' said O'Neill. 'I think he [Douglas] was trying to separate anybody who was involved.' That's not quite the impression of Frank Rijkaard, the Barca manager: 'Some of my players were a bit nervous, but Barcelona didn't start it.'

OK, but why were some of the players nervous? If – and of course it's pure speculation – Motta was having a go at one of his own players one can understand the rest would have been nervous in case they were next on the list. Or had they been watching the video of *Braveheart*, and been expecting Celtic to lay about them with claymores? We may never know. What was plain for all to see, four minutes into the second half, was Barca striker Saviola lashing out at Celtic's Thompson. That earned Barca another red card, reduced the evening's entertainment to nine men playing ten and gave Celtic a 1–0 win. Rijkaard explained afterwards that when Saviola tried to hack Thompson to pieces it was only because he 'was nervous'. A fortnight later, Celtic held Barca (missing the nervous Motta and Saviola) to a goalless draw in the Nou Camp and went through to the next round. Obviously 'nerves' are no longer the preserve of genteel Victorian ladies in crinolines.

The Egil Has Flown

Rangers lose a striker, 2004

Humility in a sportsman is a fine thing and, if it's one of those rare days when you believe something you've read in the tabloids, not often to be found in a premiership soccer player. But in March 2004 the Norwegian striker Egil Ostenstad may have taken candid self-appraisal just a little too far.

Egil left his Norwegian club, Viking Stavanger, for pastures more attractively green-backed in 1996 and, by 2003, found himself included in some interesting negotiations between his current club, Blackburn Rovers, and Glasgow Rangers. Blackburn wanted to acquire the services of Barry Ferguson from Rangers, and Egil was put into the equation as ballast. Rangers needed him as a squad player to provide cover in case of injury to either of their regular strikers, Steve Thompson and Ronald de Boer. It would be cheering to report that he seized his chance with both hands but this, alas, is not quite the case. He made four starts and came off the bench thirteen times but netted only two goals – one against St Johnstone and the other against Forfar Athletic, neither of whom could be said to have defences that would deter a part-time bank robber. He did turn out in one old-firm encounter against Celtic, and in a couple of Champions League matches, but as Rangers lost the lot that did little for his reputation.

So when, towards the end of their unsuccessful 2003–4 season, Rangers had a clear-out, Egil found himself on the road out of Scotland. Manager Alex McLeish was the soul of tact. 'It didn't quite work out for Egil,' he said, 'and we have reached an agreement which allows him to leave the club now.' (In other words, 'On your way, mate.') If he was correctly reported, Egil, on the other hand, displayed a quite startling candour: 'I'm no good,' he told the *Observer*. 'I'd advise any clubs who want me to look for someone else. If a club does want me, maybe the other players could use me as a cone in training.' With advertising copy like that, even Del-boy Trotter would have a problem finding a buyer for Egil in Peckham market, and, if his agent had hair before, he's certainly tugged it all out by now. Then again, if rumour's to be believed maybe Egil knew what he wanted all along – to return to a quiet life with Viking Stavanger and help them set out the cones for training.

Tinkerman Does a Moonie

Monaco v Chelsea, semi-finals, European Champions Cup, 2004

'Tinkerman', the press dubbed Claudio Ranieri, for his habit of fiddling with his combinations and unzipping his substitutes in public. But, like Chelsea fans and the general public, they had plenty of sympathy for him. All season long the new czar of Chelski, Roman Abramovich, had taken little trouble to conceal his desire for another manager despite the fact that Chelsea were a comfortable second in the Premiership, higher than they'd been in recent memory, and through to the knockout stages of the European Champions Cup for the first time in their history. When the unthinkable happened, and Chelsea beat high-flying Arsenal at Highbury (after sixteen previous League and Cup attempts) to go through to the semi-finals of the competition, the media could hardly find adequate superlatives to heap on Ranieri. Now, they delighted in publicly telling Abramovich, there was no way he could do without him.

If a week is a long time in politics, a fortnight is all eternity to a journalist. It took only fourteen days for the press adulation to be turned on its head and the scorn to flow. The occasion that triggered it was the first leg of Chelsea's semi-final away to Monaco, who were reckoned to have a strong defence but a relatively weak attack.

First legs are always tricky affairs, with both sides desperate not to lose or, if they must, at least to register an away goal to help tilt the balance in later tight permutations. So, when Hernan Crespo scored to equalise Monaco's opening goal from Dado Prso, Chelsea were happy to reach half-time all square at 1–1. The clangers began to be dropped – indeed scattered with something approaching prodigality – with only twenty minutes left to hold out. First, the Swiss referee fell for a shameful piece of play-acting by Chelsea's Makalele that could lead to a contract with the National Theatre when he hangs up his boots. After a bit of lightweight pushing and shoving with Monaco's Zicos he fell to ground as though he'd done a round or two with Lennox Lewis, rising from his apparently terminal injury with alacrity once Zicos had been dismissed and told never to return.

This was the cue for 'tactical anarchy'. With Monaco down to ten men, the scores level and a precious away goal in the bag, Ranieri then carried out a series of lightning substitutions that pulled defenders off the field and flung attackers onto it, apparently at random. What Chelsea now had was summed up rather neatly by Giles Smith in *The Times* as 'a defence comprising one legitimate full back, three paceless central defenders and an attack consisting of three centre-forwards, each of whom has no idea what the others are meant to be doing'. Monaco's ten men surveyed the confusion unfolding before their eyes, realised the right side of the field was effectively undefended and hot-footed down it to score twice and help themselves to a virtually unassailable 3–1 lead.

'The Mad Marauder', the press promptly dubbed Ranieri, who admitted afterwards that 'we lost the plot'. But was Tinkerman actually playing a game of consummate deviousness? Only a day or two earlier the Spanish journal *Marca* had quoted him as saying, among a number of other provocative things, 'Abramovich knows nothing about football.' Which may well be true, but not the most tactful line to take if you are hoping to hang on to a well-paid job rather than stroll off into the sunset with a £6 million pay-off. To cap it by blowing a European Champions Cup semi-final with the boss in the stands is, as one journalist noted, equivalent to doing a moonie in his face.

But was Ranieri hoping to stay in his job or had he already accepted the inevitable? He had told *Marca*, 'I know that I've got Abramovich's sword stuck in me already. I said all along that if I won everything I could be sacked. What has changed?' Perhaps this was Tinkerman's exquisite revenge for a winter of humiliation at his Russian master's hands. Show him what he was capable of by beating the long-time rivals Arsenal for a European semi-final spot, and then blow the whole lot up in front of his eyes.

Big Ron Puts His Mouth In It

Monaco v Chelsea, 2004

Poor old Ron Atkinson. With Claudio Ranieri doing his best to divert all the flak onto his own lonely figure (see page 140), our Ron's career of malapropisms hit the buffers in a big way on the very same night Chelsea were gifting a 3–1 victory to Monaco. Ron was commenting in his own inimitable, and occasionally comprehensible, way for ITV.

The game was over and the London link was off but not – alas for all concerned – the mike. With all the frankness for which he is renowned, Ron delivered his opinion on the performance (admittedly rather poor) of Chelsea's ageing defender, Marcel Desailly. His words were brief, very brief, and to the point. Even more to the point was that the relay was still going live to the Middle East, and viewers there understood immediately that Desailly's skin was not a gentle Caucasian pink.

Having led a sheltered life, I have never seen shit hitting a fan, though I have occasionally pondered the improbable physics of the thing. I can imagine the effects, though, and if a detailed description were needed Ron would be able to supply it. Before radio and television commentators had a chance to roll up their sleeves and assume their most hectoring tones, Ron had discontinued his association with ITV. Twenty-four hours later, as the press climbed eagerly onto their soap boxes, he resigned his column for the *Guardian* and became a sadder (certainly), wiser (probably) and poorer (to the tune of about £1 million) man. 'I am an idiot,' he said with unnecessary frankness next day, 'but not a racist. A racist is someone who won't give a black man a chance.' This was a point quickly endorsed by John Barnes, the former Liverpool and England star (who happens to be black), who was quick to stand by Atkinson.

In the late 1970s Ron had achieved fame in the early days of his managerial career by bringing three black players together at West Brom – Cyrille Regis, Laurie Cunningham and Brendan Batson – who became known as the Three Degrees and were material in improving the lot of black players in British soccer.

We shall miss Big Ron's inimitable style. Credited with the invention of his very own language, 'Ronglish', with which to describe soccer, he made a worthy successor to David Coleman and his wonderful 'Colemanballs' in *Private Eye*. Who now is going to inform us that 'the keeper was unsighted and he still didn't see it'? That 'on another night they'd have won 2–2'? That 'He is without doubt the greatest sweeper in the world. I'd say. At a guess'? Or, best of all, 'I never comment on referees and I'm not going to break the habit of a lifetime for that prat'?

Parrot Feeling Unwell: Vet Needed

Fulham v Arsenal, Premiership, 2004

Dateline: 9 May 2004.

Venue: Loftus Road, London (in use as Fulham's home ground while modernisation of Craven Cottage under way).

Occasion: Penultimate Premiership league match of 2003–4 season.

Significance: Arsenal, already champions, bidding for an all-time record of completing a Premiership season undefeated.

Pre-match Fulham quote: 'Arsenal have to lose some time, don't they? And why can't it be to us?' – Chris Coleman, Fulham manager.

Why not, indeed? Earlier in the season, with Arsenal at their fluent best and looking to dominate every side they encountered, Fulham had held them to a 0–0 draw at Highbury. Admittedly, Fulham had never looked like winning, but they took a point, thanks to inspired goalkeeping by Edwin van der Sar in what was described at the time as a 'bravura exhibition'.

But the parrot that had flown over the moon at Highbury was about to utter an agonised squawk as it lost its tail feathers at Loftus Road. Chris Coleman unwittingly contributed to the mishap when asked before the game to describe the tactics he would use. Implying that Fulham would seek to attack more than they had done in the first encounter, he said, 'I won't be asking the lads to do so much defending.' He might have been wise to explain to his goalkeeper that he didn't mean that remark to apply to him.

It was a pretty lacklustre game. The press, in their unending quest to overegg any pudding put in front of them, had already dubbed Arsenal 'the Immortals', conveniently overlooking their defeats by Manchester United in the FA Cup semi-finals and by Chelsea in the quarter-finals of the European Champions Cup. But the Immortals, with a summer of international duty ahead of many of the players and the Championship already won, were obviously having a problem stoking up the fires of ambition. Not that Fulham seemed any more likely to find a way round, through, over or even under their defence than they had at Highbury earlier in the season. Another 0–0 draw seemed probable, and not even an interesting one at that. Not, that is, until Fulham's Martin Djetou essayed a long pass back to the rocklike guardian of the sticks, Edwin van der Sar. It was a perfectly reasonable ball, played back firmly and accurately towards his keeper, but Arsenal's precocious mid-season signing, Jose Antonio Reyes, spotted his intentions and began a hopeful chase.

The ball, meanwhile, arrived at Edwin's feet and he surveyed it with interest, pushing it this way and that with his toes like a parrot exploring a new toy in its cage. There was just time for a split-second's nostalgia for the uncomplicated hoof onto the roof of the stand that an earlier generation of English soccer players would have bestowed on the ball before Reyes arrived, bright-eyed and bushy-tailed. Scarcely able to believe his luck, he whipped the ball away from Edwin's tactile toes and popped the ball in the back of the net to register his first goal for Arsenal. It was also the only goal of the match and, apart from Thierry Henry's two-minute burst of energy in the dying moments, there never seemed any likelihood of another. Edwin was obviously sick as a parrot afterwards. It's the only honourable thing to be in such circumstances. But, since there can't be two sick parrots in one dressing room, Chris Coleman went porcine and announced that he was as sick as a pig. With so much animal sickness around, the queue at the vets will be longer than ever.

A Towering Disaster

2004 – and on into
the future

I hate to ask this, but somebody's got to (to be candid, many already have, but don't expect self-recrimination from any quasi-governmental body). How is it that the rugby boyos can build superb new arenas the nation can be proud of, such as Cardiff's Millennium Stadium or the reinvented Twickenham, and yet we can allow such a pig's ear to be made of Wembley? The money generated by rugby is good, but only a fraction of that made by soccer. The answer, of course, is that the outstanding stadia, including those of our more imaginative and businesslike soccer clubs, are the product of private enterprise. The incompetent and inexperienced hands of quangos were kept well away from their conception, financing and building.

Pause and consider, if only in outline, the bungling that's already occurred. Nobody disagrees that Wembley was old-fashioned, inconvenient and way past its sell-by date. Whether it is a good location for a new stadium is in itself a big question. Public transport to and from the area, and therefore access, is poor. It is largely dependent on a creaking underground system in which no serious investment was made for decades, and one that is dominated by a union so backward-looking it makes steam trains look modern. But, since Wembley was the choice, we are entitled to ask many questions.

- Why, for example, is it costing so many millions of pounds more to build than the Millennium Stadium, the cost of which was £134 million *including* the property purchase?

- Why did it take the politicians so many years to decide on a national stadium?
- Why was Wembley simply closed down, several years before the decision to go ahead with a new stadium – wherever it was to be located – was taken, and before any financing had been agreed? Nobody needs reminding that no Cup finals or international matches have been staged there since 1999, thereby forfeiting an invaluable revenue stream that could have contributed millions to the new project.
- And why, having at last got round to knocking down the old stadium, are the original costs now spiralling out of control?

In February 2004 the Public Accounts Committee issued its report into the whole affair. It made sorry reading as it recounted a story of incompetence and bungling. No less than £161 million of public money had *so far* been sunk into the project. Sport England, the notorious quango behind the project, chipped in with £120 million of lottery cash. To try to counter the cost overruns, the number of seats in the new stadium has been reduced for the second time. As for the idea that the politicians foisted on the planners – that there should also be facilities for international athletics – that is fast disappearing into the ether. To all intents and purposes, the public money is gone for good, since any profits made – one long day in the future – will go to the FA, who are responsible for meeting the cost overruns. They should just about be able to bear them, so long as the money isn't frittered away on supporting the lifestyles of too many undertalented and vastly overpaid players. What a long way we've come from Lord Kinnaird and Fatty Foulke!

Postscript: Right, That's a Red Card, and Your Next Game's at the Tower!

An historical discovery, 2004 & 1526

One morning in February 2004, an unsuspecting public awoke to the news that researchers at Southampton University had unearthed a document ordering new shoes for King Henry VIII. The writing was a bit wobbly but there on the list, in unmistakeable black and white, were football boots, one pair, king, for the use of.

Why Southampton University, incidentally? Had Henry VIII given himself a free transfer to the Saints in the hope of currying favour with the Pope during his spot of bother with the pontiff? Indeed, had we got it wrong all these years? Was the break with Rome nothing to do with religion after all, but the result of a football fracas? Had the Pope excommunicated bluff King Hal for fielding unregistered heretics in an away game against Vatican City RCFC?

Perhaps the headmaster of St Paul's who, in 1581, thought it was time to find a 'trayning master' for the boys (see page 2) was not breaking new ground after all, but simply following royal precedent established fifty years earlier. And if the rotund, not to say bulky – well, all right, then, fat – monarch played football, what position did he adopt? He was hardly a flying winger with a dazzling sidestep, and as a striker he'd have had to be helped up a stepladder to nod the ball into the corner of the net. A stopper centre-half, perhaps? It would have wasted precious seconds to run all the way round him, and he certainly had a commanding presence in more senses than one. Dancing rings round the king was not the best way to win promotion, and if you beat him in the air he could easily solve the problem by removing your head.

On the whole, though, the goal seems the ideal position for Henry VIII. For a start, opponents would have had only half the goal to aim at, and, since Henry made all the rules that anyone needed to know, he would almost certainly have decreed a smaller goal at his end. Perhaps Fatty Foulke (see page 11) was not a one-off after all. Perhaps he too was following a royal precedent buried deep in the nation's folk memory.

Clearly, historians have a whole new ball game to investigate. Was the battle of Flodden in 1513 between the English and the Scots not a knights-in-armour job at all, but the first international match ever to be played? Is the reason the Scots still chunter away about the outcome because the English turned up with too many men, and their skipper, James IV, had to be stretchered off before the final whistle? And what was *really* behind all those sudden away fixtures at the Tower of London ground, supervised by an axe-wielding referee? Had Thomas More and Thomas Cromwell bundled Henry VIII into the net without the ball and been red-carded? Cardinal Wolsey got away with it only by expiring in a dugout near the Leicester City ground at Filbert Street just before he was due to appear before the one-man (Henry) disciplinary committee. And what about Anne Boleyn and Catherine Howard? Had they been caught playing an early version of *Footballer's Wives?* There's a future TV sitcom in there somewhere. Blackadder, where are you?